You Can Believe This!

Dr. John Thomas Wylie

authorHOUSE®

AuthorHouse™
1663 Liberty Drive
Bloomington, IN 47403
www.authorhouse.com
Phone: 1 (800) 839-8640

Published by AuthorHouse 11/09/2018

ISBN: 978-1-5462-6768-3 (sc)
ISBN: 978-1-5462-6767-6 (e)

*Scripture quotations marked NIV are taken from the Holy
Bible, New International Version®. NIV®. Copyright ©
1973, 1978, 1984 by International Bible Society. Used by
permission of Zondervan. All rights reserved. [Biblica]*

Print information available on the last page.

*Any people depicted in stock imagery provided by Getty Images are
models, and such images are being used for illustrative purposes only.
Certain stock imagery © Getty Images.*

This book is printed on acid-free paper.

CONTENTS

PREFACE

I write in the midst of theological training, christian, ministerial, pastoral experiences and my divine, devout, reverential encounter with divinity. For Christ I live and for Christ I will die. That is the story of my life (To direct others to the acceptance of Jesus Christ as Lord and Saviour). I am concerned about those persons who miss the mark or the life changing impact Jesus Christ could bring on their lives in accepting and following Him.

Most people who do not believe the Bible have not or do not read the Bible. People from all walks of life have read and studied the Bible and accepted Jesus Christ somewhere in the process of their life experience. I Dare You Today to read the Bible and Try Jesus' Way in your life. Only Jesus Christ can make a difference in your life; Jesus is "The Way, The Truth and The Life." The Messages you read in this little book, I hope will be an inspiration to you. The Choice is Yours to: "Believe It Or Not." I hope you will believe! This publication addresses a few messages I have spread over a library of

21 books prior; but provides some answers of concern present in this book.

The Purpose of this book is to encourage the reading and studying of "The Bible" and to take the message of Jesus Christ seriously for incorporation into your personal life. The Only Bible truly valuable to anyone is a read Bible.

Believe This!

"The Son of man is come to seek and to save that which was lost." "Thou will call his name Jesus: for he will save his people from their sins."

I Thank God that Jesus Christ is my Saviour. I had trespassed, sinned - I was lost, making a course for hell, yet in his wondrous, glorious grace Jesus saved me and made me his child. How would you view him? It is safe to say that he is the Saviour of the world, or would he say he is your Saviour? Is Jesus Christ your very own personal Saviour? Now is your time, your moment of decision. I pray you will make Jesus your choice.

Reverend Dr. John Thomas Wylie

CHAPTER

ONE

The Holy Bible

The Bible is the world's Best Seller, as everyone knows. It has been translated into more languages and dialects than any other book. Yet, the Bible is not read as often or with as much understanding and appreciation as its wide distribution might suggest. Many Bibles and Testaments lie on tables and shelves, unread and unused, sometimes brought out or dusted up to impress a guest.

But the Bible that is truly valuable to anyone is a read Bible. Our Bible is not an amulet, a magical charm, but a book to be read, marked, inwardly digested, and translated into life.

The Bible is not easy to read and understand. Many a person started out to read it, with good will and noble intentions, only to become bogged down in difficulties not of his own making. Mortimer J. Adler once wrote: "The problem of reading the Holy Book-if you have faith that it is the Word of God – is the most difficult problem in the whole field of reading... The Word of God is obviously the most difficult writing men can read. The effort of the faithful has been duly proportionate to the difficulty of the task.

Some of our difficulties in reading the Bible arise from the fact that it is, as Adler says, a holy book. The Old Testament is the sacred book of Judaism, and we Christians look upon the Old and New Testaments together as our Scripture. To us it is in some manner divine in its origin, and authoritative for our belief, worship, and life. We have to face the fact frankly, however, that various branches of Christendom and individual Christians have various ways of understanding the divine origin and authority of the Bible, and varied ways of interpreting it (J. Hyatt, The Heritage Of Biblical Faith, 1964).

Why Read The Bible?

When we look all the more unmistakably at the Bible, we discover it in every case firmly associated with a religious faith. For what reason should men do good, and stay away from evil? The Bible says it is on the grounds that the God of justice and love demands it, and needs man to be such as himself. Where does man discover the inspiration toward the good? The Bible says he doesn't discover it inside his natural desires, however it might be said of gratitude toward the God who made him and everlastingly redeems him (through the person of Jesus Christ).

We should read it since it is our Scripture in which we discover a record of what God has done all through history for his chosen people; and for humankind, and of what God expects of men because of what he has done that they might be saved.

We should read it all together that we may have an experience with the God who reveals himself as Sovereign Love, as our Creator and Redeemer, as Judge and Saviour. We find reflected in it the encounters of numerous sorts of men - some were resolved and insubordinate and rejected God's demands and his way, and some responded in faith and dutifulness. Some misjudged him, or comprehended him just in little part; others saw him or comprehended him all the more plainly and precisely, and were faintly aware of the brilliance and enormity that would dependably be avoided their full vision, yet they were eager to tail him as they was already aware him. Along these lines, notwithstanding letting us know of the activities of God we should serve, it lets us know of a few men whose ways we may imitate, and of others whose ways we must reject.

A Written Record Needed

Be that as it may, what of the people who were absent thus did not see God's association in history or the occasions encompassing Jesus Christ's manifestation, life, passing, and resurrection! To reach all men, clearly, a composed record was required. God has offered this to us in the Bible, through which He has uncovered Himself. Trust It! Believe It!

How did the Bible come to be written? Two clear proclamations from the New Testament answer this inquiry: "Comprehend that no prescience of Scripture happened by the prophet's own translation. For prescience never had its root in the will of man, yet men talked from God as they were conveyed along by the Holy Spirit" (II Peter 1:20-21); "All Scripture is God-breathed and is useful for instructing, reprimanding, correcting and preparing in righteousness" (II Tim. 3:16). Believe It!

The Bible Was Given By Inspiration

All Scripture (Bible) began in the mind of God, not in the mind of man. It was given to man by inspiration. It is imperative to comprehend this term since its scriptural importance is not quite the same as that which men regularly use it in ordinary dialect. The Bible isn't enlivened as crafted by men. Not as the compositions of Shakespeare or Plato's works.

Inspiration, in the scriptural sense, implies that God so superintended the inspired men of Scripture that they composed what He needed them to compose and were kept from blunder in doing as such. The word inspired (II Tim.3:16) really signifies "out-breathed" by God. Inspiration applies to the final product the Scripture itself-and also to the inspired men whom God used to compose the Scripture. These men who were propelled borne along remarkably by the Holy Spirit. Since this is valid, the Bible is known as the "Word Of God."

A portion of the record contain states of mind and thoughts said that are not from God. They incorporate the expressions of underhanded and absurd men and even Satan himself. Such parts are not disclosure thusly, nor are they the words of God, yet they are recorded in Scripture by God's "Intention and Inspiration."

Trust It! Believe It!

CHAPTER

TWO

Jesus' View Of Scripture

Most essential of all is Our Lord's perspective of the Scripture. What did he consider it? How could He utilize it? In the event that we can answer these inquiries, we have the appropriate response of the manifest Word of God Himself. He is the authority for any individual who claims Him as Lord!

What was Jesus state of mind toward the Old Testament? He states decidedly, "I reveal to you reality (truth), until the point that paradise and earth vanish, not the littlest letter, not minimal stroke of a pen, will using any and all means vanish from the Law until the point that everything is fulilled" (Matt. 5:18). He cited Scripture as conclusive authority, regularly presenting the announcement with the expression, "It is written," as in His experience with Satan in the allurement in the wild (Matt. 4). Jesus talked about Himself and of occasions encompassing His life as being achievements of the Scripture (Matt. 26:54, 56).

The Most clearing underwriting and acknowledgment of the Old Testament was the point at which He pronounced with certainty, "The Scripture can't be broken" (Jn. 10:35).

In the event that, we acknowledge Jesus as Savior and Lord, it would be a logical inconsistency in wording, and oddly conflicting, on the off chance that we dismissed the Scripture as the Word of God. On this point we would be in conflict with the One whom we recognize to be the endless God, the Creator of the universe.

Some have recommended that in His perspective of the Old Testament, our Lord suited to the biases of His contemporary listeners. They acknowledged it as legitimate, so He spoke to it to increase more extensive acknowledgment for His educating, however He Himself did not buy in to the prominent view.

Grave challenges plague this proposition, be that as it may. Our Lord's acknowledgment and utilization of the specialist of the Old Testament was not shallow and unessential. It was at the core of His instructing concerning His individual and work. He would be blameworthy of grave trickiness, and quite a bit of what He educated would be founded on an error.

At that point too for what reason would He suit Himself at this one point, when on other apparently less vital focuses He abrasively neglected to adjust to the biases of the time?

This is most unmistakably outlined in His state of mind toward the Sabbath. What's more, we could ask a much more essential inquiry: How would we know, whether convenience is the guideline of task, when He is adapting to obliviousness and partiality and when He isn't.

Definitions That Are Helpful

We trust that the Bible is to be translated in the sense in which the writers expected it to be gotten by perusers. This is a similar rule one utilizes when perusing the daily paper. What's more, it is astoundingly simple to recognize interesting expressions and those announcements an essayist means his perusers to take actually.

This view is conversely with that of the individuals who don't take the Bible truly. They regularly endeavor to sidestep the reasonable goal of the words, proposing that the scriptural records of specific occasions (for example, the Fall of Man, and supernatural occurrences) are only nonfactual stories to represent and pass on significant otherworldly truth.

These possessions this view say that as reality of "Don't murder the goose that lays the brilliant egg" does not rely on the exacting factuality of Aesop's tale, so we require not demand the accuracy of scriptural occasions and records to appreciate and understand reality they pass on. Some cutting edge scholars have connected this guideline even to the Cross and the resurrection of Jesus Christ. The articulation "Taking the Bible truly," in this manner, is uncertain and must be painstakingly characterized to stay away from incredible disarray.

Another essential term we should unmistakably characterize is inerrancy. What does it mean and what does it not mean? Extensive disarray can be maintained a strategic distance from by clear definition now.

An enticement we should evade is that of forcing on the scriptural journalists our twentieth century models of logical and authentic exactness and precision. For example, the Scripture depicts things phenomenologically-that is, as they have all the earmarks of being. It talks about the sun rising and setting. Presently, we realize that the sun does not really rise and set, but rather that the earth pivots. Be that as it may, we utilize dawn and nightfall ourselves, even during a time of logical edification, since this is a helpful method for portraying what seems, by all accounts, to be. So we can't accuse the Bible of blunder when it talks phenomenologically. Because it speaks in this way, it has been clear to men of all ages and cultures.

CHAPTER

THREE

Who Is God?

I like what John said on the Isle of Patmos: "Holy, Holy, Holy Lord God Almighty, which was, and is, ans is to come..." (Rev. 4:8).

It reminds me of a childhood gospel song that says, "Holy, Holy, Holy Lord God Almighty! Merciful and mighty! God In Three Persons, blessed Trinity! In Hannah's Prophetic Prayer she prays: "There is none holy as the Lord: for there is none beside thee; neither is there any rock like our God" (I Sam. 2:2). It is the Holiness of God in which we realize that He is more than man; (a divine being other than man). There is none other holy like unto our God; for in Him like a rock, we have built a solid foundation. In His Holiness we can find reguge.

God is the Only Holy One. He is the Lord of hosts, Holy! Yes, God is Holy. When I think of who God is, I must confess that God is Holy. Holy in all He says and in all He does for humankind.

Like Isaiah, I am a wretch undone; I am unpure, unclean, and all my righteousness is as filthy rags. I am imperfect and live on the margin of human error. But God is Perfect. He is the purest of the purest. God never fails in whatever He does. He is Holy. He is Perfection and Purity. Perfect in all His attributes: Holy, Holy, Holy is the Lord our God and from Everlasting to everlasting, God is Holy.

One day during my childhood, in Clarksville, Tennessee, where my life began, I asked my mother if I could go play with a close friend who lived about two miles away but on the same street. My mother gave her permission and firmly stated, "do not get into any mischief." You see, small children (especially boys) seem to find their way into trouble from time to time.

When I arrived at my friend's house, I noticed he was very sad. His father had punished him for saying naughty words to their neighbor. But when he saw me coming, he became very happy because there were not many children to play with on the street and we were best of friends.

As the story goes, my friend told his two sisters to go play in the wood shed because we were going to play church. I didn't think anything of it and said okay. Inside the wood shed was an old tree stump upright which my friend's father was going to use for firewood. I made that old log my pulpit because it was the largest. My friend Balboa and his sisters sat down on some old logs laying in front of me.

I began to imitate the preacher of our church and my friends would laugh saying, "You're so funny," "You're so crazy," I went on acting out the part of a preacher and tried to impersonate all that I had seen the preacher do in church. I even had a large white rag for my handkerchief and was waving it high in the air. We all would laugh until tears ran down our faces.

My friend's sisters would scream out loudly, "Yes, Brother!" We would go on and on rolling on the floor of the wood shed making fun of everyone who we could remember in church. Then finally, our fun came to an end.

I heard a voice call my name. I asked my friends if one of them called my name and they all answered, No! "Just keep on preaching." Everything went along fine until I said, "Won't God make you jump up and down?" My friends replied,"Yes!" and began jumping up and down.

Then suddenly, a bright light flashed inside the wood shed, and we stopped playing church because we were afraid. We were so very afraid because we did not know what had happened and could not understand what we had seen. But one of the sisters of my friend said, "I did not see no light!" "You all are lying."

Well, from that point on my friend got angry and said, "It's all over now, let us play some more church." I said that I really did not feel like it. But because he was much larger than I was, I changed my mind. Again, we make fun of everybody at church, and if my mother had known it, she would have punished me for it. Again, we laughed and rolled all over the place.

Then I said something that I would never repeat. I said, "I'm the preacher and God is going to kick your behind if you don't shout louder.' That was a big mistake! No sooner than I made the statement, a second flash of lightning struck the log in front of me. We all ran out the wood shed. My friends left me alone and ran into their house, locking the door. I ran homeward. But, on my way home I heard the voice of God speaking to me saying - "Mock not my name, nor my people, for I am Holy. This is a saying that has been with me throughout the whole of my life. I didn't know then, but now I truly know that God is Holy.

Here are a list of Scripture which to read and study and turn over in your mind, trust it!, believe it!

God Is Holy!

"Speak unto the congregation of the children of Israel, and say unto them, Ye shall be Holy; for I the Lord your God am Holy" (Lev. 19:2).

"And Joshua said unto the people, Ye cannot serve the Lord: for He is a Holy God; He is a jealous God; he will not forgive your transgressions nor your sins" (Joshua 24:19).

"There is none Holy as the Lord; for there is none beside thee: neither is there any rock like our God" (I Sam. 2:2)

"But thou art Holy, o Thou that inhabitest the praises of Israel" (Ps. 22:3)

"God reigneth over the heathen: God sitteth upon the throne of His Holiness" (Ps.47:8)

"Let them praise thy great and terrible name; for it is holy" (Ps. 99:3)

"Exalt ye the Lord our God, and worship at his footstool; for he is Holy" (Ps. 99:5)

"The Lord is righteous in all his ways, and Holy in all his works" (Ps. 145:17)

"And one cried unto another, and said, Holy, holy, holy is the Lord of hosts: the whole earth is full of his glory" (Is. 6:3)

"I will not execute the fierceness of mine anger, I will not return to destroy Eohraim: for I am God, and not man; the Holy One in the midst of thee: and I will not enter into the city" (Hos. 11:9)

"And grieve not the Holy Spirit of God, whereby ye are sealed unto the day of redemption" (Eph. 4:30)

"And they cried with a loud voice, saying, How long, O Lord, Holy and true, dost thou not judge and avenge our blood on them that dwell on the earth?" (Rev. 6:10)

God Is Eternal

What do we mean by the term "Eternal?" Eternal means having neither beginning nor end, timeless, everlasting. Psalm 41:13 says, "Blessed be the Lord Our God from everlasting and to everlasting."

One day during the hot summer season, when I was a boy – my mother was washing clothes in the kitchen. Now, that might sound strange to us today. However, back then, the washing machine was quite different in appearance than what we know it to be today. It was a huge bowl shaped tub which stood on four wheels. It had a metal arm which extended from the tub with two rubber roller pins. It had to be cranked by hand to squeeze water from the clothes and it had a hose pipe you had to connect to the kitchen faucet to fill the tub with hot or cold water in which to wash your clothes.

Once you had washed the clothes and ran them through the ringer (a hand turned crank) to wring out the water, you would hang them out on a clothes line on the back porch or in the yard to dry.

I loved to be by my mother's side when she washed the clothes because we talked about how good the Lord Is. I would ask a host of questions and my mother would give the best answer as best as she knew how.

I was helping her one day and she asked me a question. "Son, tell me something about God." Tell me something about the Lord." "Who Is God?" I said, "God loves little children like me, and He does not like us to do bad stuff. You can not see him but He's here for us." "Very good,' replied my mother.

However, the story goes on like this: I went on to say, "And God made us, every one.' but as I was saying this, a question came to my mind. "If God made us, who made God?" At first, my mother looked as though she was angry and dropped her clothes basket full of clothes and looked at me saying, "You do not understand!" God is not like us. "He is the beginning and He is the end."

She knew I did not understand everything she would tell me about God, but she always said, "One of these days you will come to know God for yourself.' She went on to say," God is, God was, and God will always be.' Then she would say, "Before anything was, God is.' I said, mother, I feel bad." She replied to me, "That's all right, God understands." She told me to always remember God is from everlasting to everlasting which means God is Eternal.

The universe, as we know it, with its stars, comets, planets, meteorites, asteroids, the sun and moon; have been in existence for a very long time. However, God was here before the twinkling stars or the shining sun, even before the moon which glows at night. God is from everlasting to everlasting, Eternal.

Before Asteroids and meteorites zoomed across the heavens, colliding with one another, there is God. More eternal than infinite galaxies and constellations is the Eternal God. Before there were a when or where, or a here or there, there is God. Before twinkling stars hung in their silver sockets, there is God. Before angels sang hymns in heaven, before there was a place called earth, there is God.

At best, we can say that even creation was a very, very long time ago, so, before pre-history there is God. God was before creation, before all things including all that we are able to comprehend about life, heaven and earth, God is before them. God is before all cycles of events which we call time. God made time for man, but God is a timeless God – for God is Eternal.

Again, we might express in some words the idea that creation was a long time ago, but God is here before time. God is timeless, above and beyond time and can not be measured by our comprehension of time; for God is Eternal.

Who is God? God is Eternal! - "Blessed be the Lord God of Israel from everlasting, and to everlasting" (Ps. 41"13)

Trust it – Believe it!

God Is Immutable

What do we mean by the term "Immutable?" One definition says it means not mutable; unchangeable. So we understand the word Immutable to mean unchangeable, an attribute which in the spiritual sense and usage applies only to God and is possessed by God. Our understanding here is that God is immutable or that God is the "Unchangeable God." God is the Unchanging God."

Malachi 3:6 says: "For I am The Lord, I change not.' This message: "I Change Not" reveals something to us about the fact that God is Unchanging. In the book of Malachi, and what Malachi has to say about God is based upon the Sovereignty of God. God is a father (1:6), a Master (1:6), a Great King (1:14). He is a Heavenly Governor (1:7,8). He gives covenants and commandments (2:4,5; 2:10;4:4). He is a sin hating God, and His people are careless, indifferent, and sinful etc., God must mete out judgment (2:2,3, 12, 3:1-5; 4:1). but because He is a God of infinite grace, He will exercise loving kindness if only His people will hear His voice and turn from their wicked ways (3:7,10-12). The dread day of the Lord shall come (3:2, 4:1,5), but the righteous need not fear, for God cares for His own (3:16, 17; 4:2,3). A righteous God never changes; His attitude toward sin for judgment, however, long delayed, will surely be carried out.

God is unchanging in that He does good to all men and women. He blesses both the good and the bad with His goodness. He allows us to live and provides for us from day to day whether we are good or bad. Everything we enjoy, everything we have comes from God who is well able to provide for all – whether we acknowledge this fact or not. God keeps on blessing us with His many blessings. Therefore, God is "Unchanging" in all that He does for us. God doesn't ever change, God is a Good God, that's why we should ever praise His Name. God has said of himself: "For I am The Lord, I change not (Mal. 3:6). God Is: "The Same Yesterday, Today, and For ever. (Heb. 13:8).

God Is A Divine Person

The word "Divine" is a term ascribed only to God. The term "Divine" describes the very nature and character of God. It tells us that God is a "Divine Person.' God thinks thoughts which are all-knowing and all-wise. He knows, He understands what we are going through in our daily lives. He feels our hurt and suffering. He hears every word that is uttered by us. He sees ever moral and immoral act. He acts and He reacts. He responds to our beckoning call. He responds according to His own will. He loves, cares, provides, and protects us each and every day. He is a Divine Person (God) at all times. He said of Himself: "I AM THAT I AM" (Exodus 3:14).

God Is Spirit

He is not visible but invisible – not natural but a supernatural being. He is not a natural person but a divine person; not of limited capabilities or attributes as man (who is limited); but of unlimited capabilities and unlimited attributes. God is a Spirit, invisible to us but becomes very real in our lives. God is "The Supreme, Divine, Personal Spirit, absolute and perfect in all His ways. He is the true and the Living God! The Scripture says in John 4:24: "God is A Spirit; and they that worship Him must worship him in spirit and in truth."

God Is Omnipotent

"Omnipotent" means all-powerful, absolute authority, unlimited in authority, possessing absolute authority; unlimited in power, possessing all-power. So we understand that "God is all-powerful.' No one will know anyone more powerful than God.

Nebuchadnezzar thought he had power, but his empire fell and crumbled. The Caesar's of the Roman Empire thought they possessed power, but in God's own time, they fell under the powerful hand of God. Alexander the Great thought he could conquer the world but soon his empire fell. These are examples of some men who thought they possessed great power. These are men who thought they were unstoppable monarchs, kings or rulers, not acknowledging a higher and greater power than themselves – The All-Powerful God.

Pharaoh of Egypt, a hard hearted man, held the children of Israel in bondage, and God sent Moses to Pharaoh saying, "Let my people go."

When Pharaoh finally let the people go, he then hardened his heart and refused to let them go. Pharaoh thought he had power because he possessed great armies and he had conquered many lands. God is more powerful than man and his armies. God is All-Powerful and manifested His power in a pillar of a cloud to lead the way; and a pillar of fire by night (Exodus 13:17-22).

The All-Powerful God was with Israel and before them leading the way. Pharaoh's army continued to pursue after the Israelites. Trapped by the Red Sea on one side and Pharaoh's army on the other side, the Israelites were sure to die. But God the All-Powerful caused the sea to go back by a strong east wind all that night, and made the sea dry land, and the waters were divided (Exodus 14;20-21). Now, that's power!

The children of Israel went into the midst of the sea on dry ground; and the waters were a wall unto them on their right and on their left. They must have been amazed by all this knowing that the All-powerful God had delivered them out of the bondage of Pharaoh's power. Pharaoh was determined to recapture the Israelites and return them to slavery. So he commanded his armies to go in after them in the midst of the sea (Exodus 14:22-23)

The All-Powerful God looked unto the Egyptians through the pillar of fire and of the cloud and troubled the host of the Egyptians (The Egyptians began to panic as their chariot wheels began to sink in the wet, spongy ground falling apart). The Egyptians said: "Let us flee from the face of Israel; for the Lord fighteth for them against the Egyptians" (Exodus 14:24-25).

And the Lord told Moses, "Stretch out thine hand over the sea, that the waters may come again upon their chariots, and upon their horsemen." Moses did as God commanded and the sea, at the command of the All-Powerful God returned to its strength and overthrew (drowned) the Egyptians. There remained not as much as one of them (Exodus 14:26-31). The All-Powerful God had delivered Israel out of the power of Egyptian bondage but executes destruction unto the ungodly (The Egyptians were ungodly).

The Babylonians, the Roman Empire, the Empire of Alexander the Great and that of Pharaoh of Egypt were all powers of men which in time had to bow down before the All-Powerful God. As I think about the Omnipotent God, I am reminded as a young boy the words of my mother as she tried to explain to me that God is All-Powerful. She did not have any theological training but she knew God. She would tell me God is All-0Powerful.

She did whatever it took to teach me along with my brother and sisters about God. She say: God is a All-Powerful being which means that God is mightier than the mightiest of men in power and strength, greater than the greatest of men, and stronger than the strongest in strength, God is the most powerful of all for He is God who is All-Powerful.

The Bible says in Jeremiah 32:17: "Ah Lord God! Behold, thou hast made the heaven and the earth by thy great power and stretched out arm, and there is nothing too hard for thee.'

Exodus 15:6 says: "Thy right hand, O Lord, has become glorious in power; thy right hand, O Lord, hath dashed in pieces the enemy."

II Chronicles 25:8 says, "God hath power to help, and to cast down.'

Psalm 29:4 says: "The voice of the Lord is powerful; the voice of the Lord is full of majesty."

God Is Omniscient

"Omniscient" means knowing all things; all-knowing. So, when we say God is omniscient, we mean God is all-knowing, for God knows all things. Those that are infinite and those that are finite, He knows all things.

In Matthew 10:29: we read these words: "Are not two sparrows sold for a farthing? And one of them shall not fall on the ground without your Father." God knows when the sparrow falls on the ground, so how much more does He know when we fall? Are not we more than the sparrow? God knows all things. God looks through eternity's window and sees the evil acts of sinful man and woman. God know the deeds of the wicked. God knows our trials, our tribulations, and our persecutions, but He take them all and works them out for the good of us all according to His divine purposes and for His glory.

Today, we live in the midst of a society where moral and spiritual values are declining, but God knows. Our society has become a growing cesspool of social injustices, family neglect, and an ever increasing crime rate, but God knows. Our society is like a parading circus of chaos and confusion, but God knows. God knows and will take care to work all matters out for the good of mankind.

God knows and does not have to second guess that which He knows. God takes the great tragedies of our lives and proves to us that: "All things work together for good to them that love God, to them who are called according to His purpose" (Romans 8:28).

In Psalm 147:5 we read: "Great is Our Lord, and of great power: His understanding is infinite."

I John 3:20 says: "For if our heart condemns us, God is greater than our heart, and knoweth all things."

God Is Omnipresent

"Omnipresent" means being everywhere at the same time, and at all times or "The state of being in an indefinite number of places at once."

Therefore, when we say God is Omnipresent, we mean that God is everywhere at all times or God is in an indefinite number of places at once.

Jeremiah 23:23: "Am I God at hand, saith the Lord, and not a God afar off?"

Matthew 28:20: "Lo, I am with you always, even unto the end of the world."

God is present with us and He is not far away but near; He is everywhere and in all places at the same time. He is with us even unto the end of the world. He is with us when we are faithful to worship Him in spirit and in truth. He is by our side when we backslide and when we sin. If we only remember that God is with us and not afar off; we would take caution as to how we live our lives, knowing that we must answer to God who is near; for we will be held accountable for our actions.

When we have done wrong (sinned) and need to repent, God is near. If we are lost in trespasses and sin and need salvation, God is Near. God is anywhere and everywhere we need Him.

Perhaps we have a son or daughter who has become a victim of drug abuse, God is near. God is near for any one who is suffering from some terminal illness. When you are experiencing a financial crisis, God is near, and not afar off. He is always present to help you if you let Him.

When you are burdened with the troubles of this world, God is Near. Perhaps we know of someone close to us – a friend, or family member who is in prison, God is near. Maybe we are one of many experiencing a failing marriage, God is near. Maybe we have some trouble on the job, God is near. Perhaps, you are seeking employment and it appears hope is no where in sight, God is near. When friends appear to have forsaken you, God is near. When the storm clouds of frustration, trials, and tribulations rage, God is near.

The strong winds of despair, sorrow, suffering, and grief may blow our way, but God is near. The lightning of calamity may strike, and the thunder of doubt may roar, but God is near. It is up to us to accept Him in the person of Jesus Christ and ask God to help us! Trust It – Believe It!

Someone has asked, "Where is God?" He's anywhere and everywhere that we may need Him. Where Is God? The Late Reverend Dr. E. W. Roberson, answered this strange question within the text of a sermon he preached entitled: "Where Is God?" A portion of that sermons reads:

"I can not see the wind, but I believe in the wind, for without the wind I smother. I believe in God. Although I can not see Him, but I can feel Him. Sometimes I can not feel the wind, but I know it is there. I can not see the Holy Spirit, but I can feel Him. Do you ever feel Him? Yes, I can feel him moving in my heart. Then, the Psalmist asked God to defend him and deliver him from the ungodly.

At this he has a strange feeling. God breaks through to you at the weakest moment. He is all right. Isn't it strange at times the silence of God seem unbearable?"

"Somebody said, "I can not see God." Well, okay. I can not see sound but I hear the rumbling. We can not see God but I know He is real (I can feel his presence). We are living in strange times. A story is told of an atheist who was teaching class one day. He wrote on the blackboard: "God is no where and left the room.'

A little took the same words and changed them to read: "GOD IS NOW HERE!"

Strange as it may seem, this suicide, this much turmoil, this distrust, this bitterness and hatred among men seem like we have switched gods.

"We exchange God for gold, grace for green backs, switched homes for houses, holy times for good times, soul sense for nonsense, church for taverns, prayers for parties, and love for hatred, but God is still in charge. Let us try to answer this atheist's question: "Where Is God?"

Firstly, God is everywhere! God is where angels bow at His feet and cry Holy. God is where the sun blazes and the stars twinkle. God is where the oceans roar and the waves leap for joy. God is where the mountains rest their brow on the bosom of floating clouds. Where the hills shout together. God is where trees grow and flowers bloom. God is where eagles soar above. God is where children play. God is in the sick rooms, and He is where wounded men lie on the Jericho road. God is on life's dangerous highways. Where Is God? God is in the church blessing the peacemaker. God is in the church blessing those who are persecuted for righteousness sake. God is in Heaven, where angels veil their faces and feet and cry Holy, Holy, Holy.

Note: "Where Is God" (Sermon): Used By Permission Via The Late Reverend Dr, E. W. Roberson, Pastor Alpha United Baptist Church, Nashville, Tennessee, 1993, 1994.

God is Omnipresent. He is present and not afar off. He is everywhere, in all places, at all times. His Presence brings peace where there is confusion. Joy where there is sorrow. God is present everywhere! His Presence brings understanding where there is ignorance and Healing where there is sickness, as well as love where there is hatred. Yes, Our God is Everywhere, and always near, and wherever and when ever we need Him. It is up to us to call on Him!

CHAPTER

FOUR

The Doctrine Of God

God created man and woman (Adam and Eve) in his own likeness. This distinguished man and woman from all other creatures God created in that God communicated a life to man and woman which did not enter that of lower animals. Unlike lower animals which act by instincts, man and woman were endowed with a spirit, self-consciousness, self-determination, and the capacity to live holy and walk in perfection. Man and Woman are the highest order of all creatures set apart with characteristics and attributes which belong to no other creatures.

God created man and woman with a free will. Free will means unrestricted in one's ability to make choices between good and evil. God provides man and woman with the power to live holy lives in fellowship and harmony with God, worshiping, obeying and trusting only God. Man and Woman are creatures dependent upon their creator as servants of God.

In the Genesis Story of Creation, we see the creature (Adam and Eve) exalting itself against the creator when they voluntarily violated the only restriction (law, command) God placed on them. They were not to eat the fruit of the tree of knowledge of good and evil. For in the day that they eat of it, they shall surely die (Denesis 2:17). The serpent (devil) persuaded Eve to take of the fruit; and Eve persuaded Adam to taste also (Genesis 3).

Both Man and Woman were deceived by the serpent to believe they would be like God, knowing good and evil, never dying. When the man and woman looked upon creation they saw themselves as lords of creation; but when they looked to God they saw themselves as his servants. Satan (the devil, serpent) said: "Ye shall be as gods" (Genesis 3:5). Following the serpent's deception, they both fell from fellowship with God. They fell from holiness and perfection. They lost it all. Their spiritual death was immediate (lost in sin), and their physical death would eventually come.

Man and woman were perfect and holy as long as they kept their eyes on God, but because they disobeyed God; becoming servants of the devil, they have brought upon themselves imperfection, shame, despair, carnal-mindedness, and rebellion against God. By their disobedience sin is passed on to all mankind. This tells us that life has no purpose or meaning apart from God.

God in His infinite wisdom created man and woman for the purpose of love and fellowship. He communicated with them daily. God intended all things to be good. He wanted man and woman to return their love, loyalty, and reverence unto Him. But they chose to rebel instead of returning love (disobedience).

God still is like a father who pitieth his child. He still seeks to love and fellowship with mankind reaching out through His own self-disclosure of Himself and His purposes to the comprehension of mankind.

The Late Reverend Dr. John F. Grimmett, American Baptis College, Nashville, Tennessee states in his book, "God and His Self-Revelation To Man," 1980: "The presupposition of Revelation is that God is hidden from man's view. Revelation, therefore, is God's unveiling, uncovering, disclosing of Himself and His purposes to the comprehension of man" (I Sam. 3:21; Isa. 22:14; 40:5; 53:1).

Historically, men and women have sought to satisfy the soul's craving desire to worship a power or deity. God reaches out to humanity voluntarily as He reveals Himself and his purposes to mankind. God's revelation or disclosure of Himself to humanity climaxes in the Person of Jesus Christ. Those who accept Jesus Christ as Lord and Saviour of their lives are brought back into the fellowship of God their Father. God further reveals Himself through His written but inspired Word, the "Bible." Humans need to find purpose and significance in their lives is rooted in God's self-disclosure of Himself through the Scriptures of the Bible; and as fore stated climaxes in the Person of Jesus Christ, His example, His life, and His teachings.

As a result of God's redemptive power, the redeemed (the church) of God are bound together as a body of baptized believers in Jesus Christ, proclaiming what God has done for humanity in the person of Jesus Christ as they are led by the Holy Spirit of God.

Although the believer does not know all the future, He does know one day we all will be like Jesus Christ. We shall see Him as He is and live in perfect fellowship with Him. The Same Christ who died on Calvary's Cross in our place, for the redeeming of our sins, rose up and ascended on high and has gone to prepare a place for us in Heaven.

CHAPTER

FIVE

Who Is Jesus Christ? Jesus Is A Divine Person

The word "Divine" is a term ascribed only to God. This term describes the very nature and character of Christ. It tells us that Jesus Christ is a Divine Person. Jesus is God at all times.

Jesus said of Himself: "If ye had known me, ye should have known my Father also: and from henceforth ye know Him, and have seen him (John 14:7)." "He that hath seen me hath seen the Father (John 14:7)." "No man can say that Jesus is the Lord, but by the Holy Spirit" (I Corinthians 12:3)." Jesus said that He is God and this is revealed to us by the Holy Spirit. Jesus said: "I and my Father are one" (John 10:30).

Jesus Christ Bears Witness Of His Divinity

Divinity is a term which means a Divine Person, God. Jesus Christ bears witness of his divinity when He says: "I am the light of the world..." (John 8:12). However, the Pharisees who heard Jesus make this claim began to dispute Him saying: "...Thou bearest record thyself; thy record is not true" (John 8:13). Jesus said to them: "...though I bear record of myself, yet my record is true: for I know when I came, and whither I go; but ye cannot tell whence I come, and whither I go" (John 8:14).

"Ye judge after the flesh, I judge no man." "And yet I judge, my judgment is true; for I am not alone, but I and the Father that sent me" (John 8:15-16). "It is also written in your law, that the testimony (witness) of two men is true" (John 8:17). "I am one that bear witness of myself, and the Father that sent me bearest witness of me" (John 8:18).

No doubt, the Pharisees did not believe Jesus. In John 8:19 they ask Jesus: "Where is thy Father?" Jesus answered: If Ye had known me, ye should have known my Father also."

Jesus spoke to them again, saying: "I go my way, and ye shall seek me, and shall die in your sins: whither I go, ye cannot come" (John 8:21).

The Jews thought that Jesus would commit suicide (see John 8:22). Jesus said to them: "Ye are from beneath; I am from above: ye are of this world; I am not of this world."

"I said therefore unto you, that ye shall die in your sins: for if ye believe not that I am he (that is to say, God), ye shall die in your sins" (John 8:23,24).

Jesus Is A Human Person

Jesus possessed a human nature as well as a divine nature (The God-Man). The Bible declares in John 1:1, 2: "In the beginning was the Word, and the Word was with God, and the Word was God." "The same was in the beginning with God.' Then in John 1:14, we read: "And the Word was made flesh, and dwelt among us (and we beheld his glory, the glory as of the only begotten of the Father) full of grace and truth."

Jesus Christ was born into this world of an earthly mother, but without an earthly father. God manifested Himself in the womb of the Virgin Mary (by His Spirit, The Holy Spirit) whom Joseph, Mary's earthly husband had not known.

"And the angel said unto her, Fear not, Mary: for thou hast found favor with God. And Behold, thou shalt conceive in thy womb, and bring forth a son, and shalt call his name Jesus. He shall be great, and shall be called the Son of the Highest: and the Lord God shall give unto Him the throne of His father David; (human lineage) And he shall reign over the house of Jacob forever; and of His Kingdom there shall be no end" (Luke 1:30-33). "For with God nothing shall be impossible" (Lukie 1:37).

Jesus Christ is God Incarnate (100% God And 100% Man) who took on human flesh and experienced our suffering (human); while still God (Divine) who overcomes our suffering. (Study the terms God-Man and Incarnate in A Bible Dictionary).

Jesus' Message Summarized

"For the Son of man is come to seek and to save that which was lost" (Luke 19:10). The character and purpose of Jesus Christ as Saviour are the main theme of Luke's writings. The activity and teachings of Jesus in the Gospel of Luke are focused on lifting men out of their sins and bringing them back to life and hope, The miracles, the parables, the teachings, and the acts of Jesus Christ exemplify his redemptive power and call.

The concept of Jesus as the Son of Man emphasizes his humanity and his compassionate feeling for all men. He was to be a light to lighten the Gentiles, and the glory of... Israel" (Luke 2:32).

The Fullness Of Time

The old legend about the center of the world is, therefore, truer than the men who invented it realized. It was no haphazard that made Bethlehem and Nazareth or Calvary the cradle of the Christian Faith. It was the best possible place for the launching of a world religion (Stewart, 1959).

"But if the place God chose was ideal for the coming of the Christ, the time God chose was ideal too; and it is this we are now to consider. It was when the fullness of time was come, says Paul, that God sent forth His Son (Gal. 4:4). That is to say, it was when world conditions were exactly ripe that God's supreme revelation in history came. It was when all the factors – social, economic, moral, religious had converged upon him that the man of God's right hand came forth" (Stewart, 1959).

"Search the pages of history up and down, and in all the tale of the centuries you will not find any generation in which Christ could better have come than just the generation in which He did come. "There is a tide," says Shakespeare, "in the affairs God; and it is when that tide reaches the flood, when all the preparatory work is done and world conditions are clamoring for it and human souls are open, it is then, at the flood-tide hour of history, that God launches his new adventure" (Stewart, 1959).

The Political Preparation

"When Jesus Christ first came, it was the fullness of the time politically. What was the dominating feature of the political situation of the generation to which Jesus Christ came? It was the unification of the world. That was Caesar's achievement. The day of closed frontiers was over. The day of separate, self-sufficient, antagonistic nations, gazing suspiciously at one another across bristling defenses, was done. All the way from the Atlantic to the Caspian, from Britain to the Nile, from Hadrian's Wall to the Euphrates, the Roman standards could be seen. Everywhere the barriers were down. The chaos had been welded and consolidated into a community. The world was one big neighborhood. Three factors contributed to this situation in which the gospel of Jesus Christ was born.

One was Roman peace. If Jesus Christ had come a few centuries later, he would have found civilization too preoccupied with its terrible struggle against the barbarian hordes from the North to have any ear for the gospel. But Jesus Christ came to a generation when the Roman peace held the world, held it no doubt with an iron hand, but held it sure and far-flung and broken; and men could hear the Bethlehem angels sing" (Stewart, 1959).

"A Second element making for the solidarity of the world when Jesus Christ came was the colossal streets. From end to end of the domain the considerable interstates ran, triumph of Roman designing. The ten-thousand workers in the sweat of their foreheads little thought they were setting up a path for the Son of God. Be that as it may, they were. Along these magnificent lines of correspondence, worked to convey Caesar's legions to each edge of domains, the evangelists of the gospel came walking; and all around their message spread like a fierce blaze. Jesus Christ's men could never have proselytized the world as they did had it not been for the Roman roads" (Stewart, 1959).

"The Third component making the world solidarity when Jesus Christ came was dialect. Picture what might have happened if the principal ministers or disciples had hinderances of dialect to battle with. Their development would have been backed off and appallingly hindered, in numerous spots conveyed to a halt, and that at a stage in their incredible enterprise when it was totally basic to lose no time.

In any case, as it seemed to be, wherever they went they found there was one dialect that helped them through. For while every position still had its own tongue or lingo, all over the place the general population were bilingual and all knew Greek.

In the statures of Galatia as much as in the city of Athens, in Spain as in Rome, the teachers could communicate in Greek realizing that they would be caught on. The Roman peace, the immense streets, the basic dialect – these were the things that had connected the world into one major neighborhood thus had arranged the path for Jesus Christ."

The Economic Preparation

"At the point when Jesus Christ came, it was the completion of the time politically, as well as monetarily. Where it counts underneath the sparkling society of that old world, down underneath its extravagance and radiance, distress was fuming and neediness strolled in clothes. Two men of each three in the city of Rome were slaves, negligible merchandise and belongings; and now and again the slave heart revolted. When the considerable artists of Rome sang of the Golden Age, it was by and large to the past that they turned their eyes. Not for them, with respect to the Hebrew prophets, did the Age of Gold lie in front, sparkling in a cheerful, enticing future; the Golden Age of bounty lay behind them, and it was the Age of Iron at this point."

"Surely, in numerous quarters of Caesar's territories the monetary circumstance had achieved the purpose of emergency when

Jesus Christ came. So it was in Palestine. The deplorable outcome of war, the wild, giant excess of Herod the Great, the weight of tax assessment, both common and religious, the developing over-population which made it unthinkable for the area to give sustenance enough to its own particular tenants – these things had hastened a time of unexampled dejection among the considerable majority of the people."

Life had developed consideration ridden and loaded with stress. Tension for the morrow was composed profound upon men's appearances and on their souls, and the majority of the world appeared to be tangled and turned out badly. It was rang out in Galilee; and men's hearts jump up and tuned in, for the totality of time had come."

The Moral Preparation

"At the point when Jesus first came, it was the completion of time ethically. Swinburne in one of his lyrics shouts out protestingly that after Jesus Christ the world has never known the same merriment again; that Jesus Christ has taken all its characteristic joy and great spirits away; that until then Greco-Roman had been flawlessly cheerful and blameless and placated in its temperament adore, it love of Zeus and Dionysus and Aphrodite, that Jesus Christ truly ruined everything." Thou hast conquer'd, O pale Galilean; the world has developed dark from Thy breath.'

"Yet, all that is false to the realities. Verifiably it is rubbish. The thought of an old world glad and pure and carefree and ethically settled is basically a myth. If you need the genuine truth about the world, you will get it, not in Swinburne, but rather in Paul, in that awful picture that stands perpetually for every single future age to peruse in Paul's first part to the Romans – a world that was soaked in good sadness. "The world was developing old," says Mommsen," and not even Caesar could make it youthful once more.' No, in fact! For it had trespassed its childhood away, and all the freshness of the dew of youth was gone, and just the worm, the infection, and the despondency were cleared out.

All over the best spirits were in gloom. All over the noblest souls it appeared that the entire world was seeking after its crazy path down to catastrophe and obscurity and extreme night. It was then that Jesus Christ came, going in the significance of his strength and made the old world new."

"Might we not say that some such effect of the spirit of Jesus Christ upon the ethical existence of men and countries is one of the prime needs of today?" When the analysis of loosening profound quality and messing with codes of honor has been conveyed to a specific point, unavoidably there comes a response. Unavoidably that something of God which hides underneath the surface of men's souls stands up and records its challenge.

The allure of the dramatist statement of faith and the bait of the current good news of uncontrol have the living Jesus Christ to figure with. Men won't be fulfilled by the morals of the dust dependably. They are growingly insubordinate against them now. In the ethical circle the totality of the time has come.

The Religious Preparation

"When Jesus Christ first came, it was the fullness of the time religiously. The old gods of Rome were either dead or dying. To fill the gap, two expedients were tried. One one hand, a whole new batch of gods was imported from the East, outlandish, oriental deities brought in to stir Rome's jaded senses – till among the philosophers the overcrowding of Olympus, where the gods were supposed to dwell, became a standing joke.

On the other hand, the strange phenomenon of Caesar worship appeared; the emperor himself was accorded with divine honors. But all expedients failed. What was a whole Pantheon of gods worth if they had nothing to say to a man with a broken heart? What could the divinity of Caesar say to a soul stabbed with the remorse of sin? When everything had been done that could be done, the hungry hearts of men were hungry still" (Stewart, 1959).

"But there were something more definite than that. There was a strange sense of something impending from the side of God. In many parts of the world men of deeper nature and more spiritual vision were peering into the darkness for some faint flush of dawn. Among the Jews themselves the hope of the Messiah was blazing more clearly than it had for centuries.

The great mass of Jewish literature from the period between the Old Testament and the New Testament is full of this great hope. And when any new voice rang out across the land, the voice of John the Baptist, for instance, immediately on every lip there rose the question - "Is this the Messiah Now?" 'The air was tense with expectation. And the Jews, penetrating as they did into every corner of the empire, took that great dream with them and handled it on. Nothing cleared the way for Jesus Christ more definitely than that passionate hope. The fullness of Time had come."

"Today in the religious sphere the same spirit is at work. On the one hand, just as in the Roman Empire, the old gods are dead or dying. The gods of convention, the gods of outworn, second-handed religious tradition, the gods of materialism and secularism, are losing grip.

And on the other hand, our generation is marked by a sudden new outbreak of interest in Jesus Christ. Witness the books about Jesus Christ that these last years have produced. Witness the fact that outside Christendom altogether, in India, for example, men are beginning to look to Jesus Christ of Nazareth for guidance.

Witness the new spiritual awakening among youth. Witness a score of similar significant facts. One thing is certain: Where Jesus Christ is concerned today, the spiritual tide is rising. And it may be our very generation is going to be the flood coming in across the ramparts of the Church and of the world irresistibly. The fullness of the time is nigh.'

"So the Redeemer came. Somewhere in the heart and mind of God from the very foundation of the earth the Christ had been waiting, hidden in the counsels of eternity until the great bell of the ages should strike; and when at last everything in the world and in the souls of men was ready and prepared, he came, the Word of God made flesh, not a moment early and not a moment late, but exactly on the stroke of the hour. It was the Day of the Lord.

"It is still the Day of the Lord, whenever another soul enthrones him. "Even so, come, Lord Jesus" (Stewart, 1959).

CHAPTER

SIX

Who Is Jesus Christ?

For centuries, men have made the inquiry: "Who Is Jesus Christ?" Who is this One who asserts the consideration of the entire world? Who is this Man who has such abiding place in the hearts of a endless a number of people?

There have been numerous perspectives about Jesus. Some have said that he was insane, that he was crazy, that he was allied with the Devil. Be that as it may, other individuals have said that he was precisely what he professed to be, Jesus Christ, the Son of the Living God.

One day He called to his disciples to him and asked them, "Whom do men say that I the Son of man am?" They replied: "Some say that you are John the Baptist; some say you are Elijah, and others say that you are Jeremiah." "However whom say ye that I am?" he asked them. What's more, this is when Peter, the representative for the gathering, stated, "Thou art the Christ, the Son of the living God." This answer incredibly satisfied Jesus, for He stated, "Flesh and blood hath revealed it unto thee, but my Father which is in heaven" (Matt. 16:16).

I couldn't educate you on everything concerning Jesus Christ. I proved unable, even in a few messages or books about him, give all of you reality or truth about the greatest person of the hundreds of years. By what means can a man cover the character of Jesus in a couple of pages of a book? We can talk about quickly and essentially a portion of the high points that answer this inquiry, "Who Is Jesus Christ?" Some of these facts were covered in chapter five but we will yet view others.

He Existed With The Father Before
The Foundation Of The World

In his incredible supplication in John 17, he discussed the glory that he had with the Father before the world started. In John 1:1 we return into the ages before the world was made, and we hear that "in the beginning was the Word, and the Word was with God, and the Word was God." When God stated, "Let us make man in our image," Jesus Christ was with him as a part of the Trinity.

Jesus Claimed To Be God

Jesus said of Himself: "He that hath seen me hath seen the Father." The exceptionally old cry of humankind has been, "Show to us the Father." Christ came uncovering the character of God.

He came saying: "I am God revealed; I am God in the flesh; I have come down to earth that man might find and know the Holy One of heaven."

Jesus Claimed To Be Able To Forgive Sins

Nobody can do that aside from God, however Jesus Christ as God took this upon himself. While Jesus was preaching one day, a man was let down in his presence from the roof top. Jesus said to the man, "Thy sins be forgiven thee." Immediately the Pharisees started to mumble, saying, "Nobody can forgive sins but God." For once they were correct. In any case, with a specific end goal to demonstrate that he was God, Jesus Christ stated, "Son, are thy sins forgiven thee, as well as now you can ascend and walk." No one can pardon sin aside from God, and Jesus forgives sin; therefore he is God.

Jesus Claimed To Merit First Place In The Lives Of Men

Jesus gave men that if they followed him, they should forsake all and love him most importantly above all. Jesus disclosed to them that He ought to be the first and the foremost in every walk of life. No negligible man can make a case for all man's dependability along these lines; yet Jesus Christ was deserving of all respect and all praise and all loyalty, for he is the divine Son of God.

Jesus Claimed To Be The Judge Of The World

This extraordinary capacity (great function) can not be asserted by anybody other than God. God has three forceful capacities - that of creation, that of conservation, and that of judgment. These three capacities were altogether asserted and practiced by Jesus Christ.

We should, along these lines, concede and acknowledge that Jesus is divine, that he is the best marvel ever. We should concede that his cases are valid, or that he is the greatest faker on the planet. We may scrutinize his godliness or uncertainty his virgin birth, yet the reality still remains that the world has never observed a man like Jesus Christ, for he is for sure the heavenly Son of the awesome Father.

A man who has a decent unadulterated spouse may scrutinize the reality of her integrity and immaculateness. Regardless of his questions, her character isn't transformed; she is still great and unadulterated. Men have questioned Jesus Christ; they have said all manner of evil things against him, however despite everything he stands the awesome Son of God.

Jesus Is God Come Down To The World In The Flesh

We read that "the Word was made flesh." To give us a chance to look at a portion of the confirmations that Jesus Christ is God.

1. The Same Names Were Used of Jesus as Were Used of God.

In Isaiah 44:6, God is talking and says: "I am the first, and I am the last.' In Revelation 22:13, we hear Jesus Christ say, "I am ..., the first and the last."

2. In the Twenty-fourth Psalm we hear this inquiry, "Who is this King of glory?" And the appropriate response returns, "The Lord of hosts, he is the King of glory.' In I Cor. 2:6 we read that "they crucified the Lord of glory." God and Jesus Christ are talked about in same terms.

3. In Romans 9:5 we read that "Jesus Christ is over all, God blessed for ever.'

***Note: In Chapter Three, God has five definite attributes - Jesus has Them All. Review Chapter Three. ***

Jesus Christ Received The Same Worship, Faith, And Loyalty Which Were Due To

God Alone

Jesus taught that men should worship God just; yet he acknowledged this love, this worship for himself. In the book of Revelation we see the redeemed hosts of paradise worshiping the Lamb even as they worshiped the Father. We read in Hebrews 1:6; "Let all of the angels worship him"; and the writer is talking about Jesus Christ. Definitely One who justifies, or merits the worship of angels and men is God himself.

CHAPTER

SEVEN

Jesus Is The Saviour Of Man

Jesus Came Into The World
For This Purpose

"The Son of man is come to seek and to save that which was lost." "Thou will call his name Jesus: for he will save his people from their sins."

I Thank God that Jesus Christ is my Savior. I had trespassed, sinned - I was making a course for hell, but in his wondrous grace Jesus saved me and made me his child. How would you view him? It is safe to say that he is the Savior of the world, or would he say he is your Savior? Is Jesus Christ your very own personal Savior? If not, at that point, so far as you are concerned, he died in vain.

Jesus is Carrying On This Work Today

In human hearts everywhere throughout the world he is working through his Holy Spirit to save men. Jesus Christ knows his people, and he is calling them by name. It is safe to say that he is calling you? Is it accurate to say that he is working in your heart? Try not to dismiss him and don't deny him, for to do as such is to die in sin.

Jesus Is Our Daily Strength

No man can really live without Jesus' help. Jesus gives us power to live. Jesus is the only One who can enable us to live as we ought to from everyday. Jesus gives that power, as each child of God can testify.

Jesus Intercedes For Us

Jesus ever lives to make intercession for us. I remember as a young boy who has three sisters, I would not approach my father to ask a favor, or get permission for something. I would ask my mother to talk to my father or I would tell my sisters. My Sisters did not mind interceding for me. So it is that when we have sinned, Jesus Christ is there closer to God the Father than anyone else, interceding for us at the throne of grace. That is what Jesus Christ is doing right now – He is making intercession for us.

Jesus Is The Coming King

When Jesus Christ returned to paradise (heaven), the men dressed in white said to the disciples: "This same Jesus... shall so come in like way as ye have seen him go into paradise." All through the New Testament this reality rings out - Jesus Christ is coming back once more! Jesus is coming noticeable all around to take unto himself forever each one of the individuals who have had faith in his supreme name. Afterward, Jesus is coming in magnificence with his holy people to rule for all eternity. Will you be embarrassed at his coming? What will you do when Jesus Christ returns?

Jesus Christ Is The World's Final Judge

At the judgment seat of Jesus Christ, he will judge work by all believers. Also, at the judgment of the considerable white throne of royalty, Jesus will judge the individuals who have let him well enough alone out their lives. Each man and woman must face one of these judgments, either to be remunerated or to be thrown out into unceasing enduring until the end of time.

Today I come to hand to you a loving invitation in this book, "You Can Believe This." You are welcome to come to Jesus Christ and to get the great things he has for his children. If you reject him, or dismiss him, in the colossal day of judgment you will be called to show up before him.

Is it accurate to ask if you are prepared for that extraordinary day to come? Is it safe to say that you are prepared to stand before Jesus Christ who died for you and whom you have rejected? "Be ye likewise prepared: for in such a hour as ye think not the Son of man cometh."

Who is Jesus? Jesus is God himself. He is a great individual. He is a Wonderful Savior. He is our every day strength - our coming King and Final last Judge. However, the primary inquiry is this: "Is Jesus your Savior Today?"

CHAPTER

EIGHT

Who Is The Holy Spirit?

Firstly, we do not refer to the "Holy Spirit" as "it" anymore than we should refer to our Lord Jesus Christ as "it." The Holy Spirit is not a thing nor object, but one who is divine. "He is the third person of the Holy Trinity, and the unseen but Omnipresent (Ever-present) and Omnipotent (All-powerful) Divine Spirit of God, present at creation (Gen. 1:2; Ps. 104:30), and given by God." (Is. 42:1-5) He is poured upon us (Is. 44;3); is a source of instruction (Neh. 9:20); of wisdom (Job 32:8); and sound judgment (Num. 11:17).

"God as present and dynamic in the spiritual encounters of men." The term in its later sense does not happen in the Old Testament. The fundamental Hebrew words mean additionally "breath" or "wind," as in the Greek. It is just as men knew about a type of presence which had no material shape or frame; the storage room relationship they could consider was that of breath or wind. Jesus himself used the relationship as a part of his discussion with Nicodemus about being "born of the Spirit" (John 3:5-8). The less God was considered as having a physical structure, the more accentuation was laid on his being "a Spirit," as undetectable however as real as the wind or breath.'

Differently called "the Spirit" (I Tim. 4;1) or the "Spirit of God" or the "Spirit of Christ," and so on. The convention of the Holy Spirit, as a component of the Trinity is to some degree in any event outside human ability to understand, and we are restricted to the announcements of Scriptures. The Scriptures exhibit the Holy Spirit as a particular identity and as a component of the 'Godhead" or "Trinity" (Matt. 3:16-17, 28:19; John 14:16-17, 15:26), and individual pronouns are used (John 16:13, 14, Acts 13:2). His divinity is in like manner underscored by providing for him names that have a place with God (Acts 5:3,4; Is. 6:9; Heb. 10:15) and divine traits are expressed as having a place with him (I Cor. 2:11, 12:11; Heb. 9:14).

The work of the Holy Spirit is absolutely critical to men. He is the prompt wellspring of life (Ps. 104:29; Job 32:8; Num. 11:17); He had impact in the happenings to Christ (Lk. 1:35; John 1:32; 3:34); and he is the revealer of divine truth. Accordingly, the wellspring of the propelled Scriptures (John 14:26; 16:13; I Cor. 2:10-13; II Tim. 3:16). This implies the Holy Spirit is dynamic in changes and in the illumination of the believer by the Word of which he is the creator (Eph. 6:17; Jn. 16:8; Acts 2:37; Acts 20:32). As a major aspect of this the Holy Spirit is said to stay in us (Rom. 8:9; I Cor. 6:19, 20; Eph. 4:30; 5:18...etc).

The Holy Spirit Is A Person

The Work of the Holy Spirit is absolutely critical to men. He is the prompt wellspring of life (Ps. 104:29: Job 32:8; Num. 11;17); he had impact in the happening to Christ (Lk. 1:35; Jn. 1:32; 3:34); and he is the revealer of divine truth. Accordingly, wellspring of the propelled Scriptures (Jn. 14:26; 16:13; I Cor. 2:10-13; II Tim. 3:16). This implies the Holy Spirit is dynamic in changes and in the illumination of the believer by the Word of which He is the creator (Eph. 6:17; Jn. 16:8-cf. Acts 2:37-Acts 20:32). As a major aspect of this the Holy Spirit said to stay in us (Rom. 8:9; I Cor. 6:19-20; Eph. 4:30; Eph. 5:18).

To The Holy Spirit is credited by the Scriptures every one of the qualities of identity.

In the Old Testament He was the accomplice of God in Creation. "The spirit of God moved upon the substance of the waters" (Gen. 1:2); and the spirit of God hath made me" (Job 33;4).

It is recorded that the "spirit of the Lord happened upon" people like Gideon (Judges 6:340 and David (I Sam. 16:13). He was distinguished in Isa. 63:10-11 as "his heavenly spirit" (lower case in the King James however promoted in NIV and others). Progressively God the Holy Spirit was being recognized as a Person.

In the New Testament, He is concurred numerous extra traits of identity that of knowing (Rom. 8:27), of feeling (Eph. 4:30), of willing (I Cor. 12:11), and all ways of individual activities, for example, hearing, talking, controlling, giving endowments." "The Holy Spirit is a divine person – Indeed one of three persons of the Godhead" (Agnew, 1980).

The Holy Spirit Is A Member Of The Trinity

How it is conceivable that there can be three persons in the Godhead (Trinity)? Deuteronomy 6:4 announces: "The Lord our God is One

Lord." However, this can be valid in the same sense that a man and a wife, one marriage, get to be one, yet stay two persons. Subsequently should a man leave his father and mother, and might cleave unto his wife" is pronounced in the Scriptures in Gen. 2:24, and embraced by Jesus Christ in Matthew 19:4, 5: "They might be one substance.' Furthermore, He is an extremely dynamic Member of the Trinity."

That there is a majority of the Godhead was hinted in the times of old with such plural distinguishing proof as "God said, Let us make man in our image, after our likeness" (Gen. 1:26, italics included), and in Isaiah's record: "I hear the voice of the Lord saying, Whom should I send, and who will go for us" (6:8)?

It would seen that it is the Second Person of the Godhead talking as He perceived the Trinity, in the announcement, "The Lord God has sent Me, and His Spirit" (Isa. 48:16). As recorded in Luke 4:18-21, Jesus is tolerating as valid with respect to himself and the Holy Spirit the announcement as recorded in Luke 4:18-21, made by Isaiah in 61:1,2, "The spirit of the Lord God is upon me, on the grounds that the Lord hath blessed me to preach great greetings unto the quiet; he hath sent me to tie up the beaten down, to broadcast freedom to the hostages, and the opening of the jail to them that are bound; to declare the satisfactory year of the Lord, and the day of retaliation of our God; to solace all that grieve.' To this Jesus included, "This day is this sacred text satisfied (fulfilled) in your ears.'

In any case, no place do we discover the prophets under the Old Covenant plainly displaying the Trinity.

It was New Testament times before the Holy Spirit was obviously recognized as a member of the Trinity. Two enchanted appearances are recorded. To Mary the blessed messenger said, "The Holy Ghost might happen upon thee, and the power of the Highest should dominate thee" (Lk. 1:35). At that point at the sanctification of Jesus Christ, the voice of God the Father originated from heaven: "This is my beloved Son, in whom I am well pleased,' and God the Holy Spirit slid 'like a pigeon, and lit upon him" (Matt. 3:16,17). Yet still the Holy Spirit was dressed in mystery – slipping like a bird.

All things considered, as the New Testament developed, it uncovered the truth of the Trinity (Godhead) which had been yet a shadow in the Old Testament. Jesus Christ plainly shows this in His awesomeness, "Sanctifying through water them for the sake of the Father, and of the Son, and of the Holy Spirit (Matt.; 28:19).

Luke perceives the Trinity in his depiction of the passing of Stephen who "being brimming with the Holy Ghost,' Luke announces, "turned upward enduringly into heaven, and saw the glory of God, and Jesus Christ remaining on the right hand of God, and said, Behold I see the heaven opened, and the Son of man sitting on the right hand of God (Acts 7:55, 56). Paul closes his second letter to the Corinthians with the "Trinitarian beatitude": "The finesse of the Lord Jesus Christ, and the adoration for God, and the fellowship of the Holy Ghost, be with all of you (II Cor. 13:14).

Spiritual Power/Profound Power

"Spiritual Power/Profound Power!" What pictures and trusts that brings before the believer's mind! For Spiritual power is an appropriate aching for God's people to have.

However, Christians may vary on the way to spiritual power, all concur that it identifies with the work of the Holy Spirit. Understanding the service of the Holy Spirit, along these lines, ought to be critical to the believer. A Christian is one who has received Jesus Christ; a profound Christian is one who shows Jesus Christ living through his life, and this is proficient by the work of the indwelling Holy Spirit.

Most profound sense of being then, is Christlikeness that is delivered by the product of the Spirit. What better representation of Jesus Christ is there than "adoration, delight, peace, persistence, consideration, goodness, loyalty, delicacy, poise" (Gal. 5:22, 23)?" These qualities portray the product of the Spirit, and they picture Our Lord. Profound power is not so much or typically the inexplicable or dynamite, but instead the reliable display of the attributes of the Lord Jesus Christ in the believer's life. This is the action of the Holy Spirit, of whom the Lord Jesus said, "He should celebrate Me.'

A comprehension of the service of the Holy Spirit is essential to Christian living. In any case, one can't completely grasp the work of a man without additionally knowing something about that person. In like manner it is important to know something about the person of the Holy

Spirit with a specific end goal to completely welcome His work. It might appear to be dull to the reader to seek after the investigation of the Spirit's identity and divinity; yet who He is foundational to what He does, and an information of both. His person and work is fundamental to Christian commitment and living. No other gathering among the totality of believers of God has ever been the recipient of so a considerable lot of the services of the Spirit as has the assemblage of Jesus Christ which started upon the arrival of Pentecost. For instance, the lasting indwelling of each believer by the Holy Spirit was not experienced before that day.

His work of joining believers to the "risen Christ" was unimaginable before the restoration of Jesus Christ and the plunge of the Spirit at Pentecost. His showing service, His solace, and His intervention are advantages that all Christians may encounter without confinement or restriction today. This is genuinely the age of the Spirit, and none of the people of God have been so incredibly special as are Christians in this age.

Paul composed one and only roundabout letter to a gathering of holy places, and that was Ephesians, which was sent to all holy places in Asia Minor. It is intriguing to notice how as often as possible he specifies different services of the Holy Spirit in this letter. It is if the Spirit were a wide range anti-microbal for the ills of persons in those holy places. Paul reminded the people who may need affirmation of their salvation that the Spirit had fixed them and His presence in their lives was the sincere, or certification, of the everlasting character of their reclamation (Eph. 1:13,14). In the event that God has put His own seal of proprietorship upon us in the person of His Spirit, then nothing can make our reclamation more secure.

The apparently unthinkable work of joining Jews and Gentiles in one body was expert by the Spirit, and this union carries with it an entrance or presentation into the very presence of the Father (Eph. 2:18). Paul promises the individuals who require the quality to give Christ a chance to rule in their lives that the Holy Spirit will give that capacity (Eph. 3:16) and when He does they can start to comprehend the measurements of the love for Jesus Christ."

The reasonable and vital issue of connections to different believers is to be guided and watched by the standard of "being steady to protect the solidarity of the Spirit in the obligation of peace" (Eph. 4:3).

One body, one Spirit, one trust, one Lord, one faith, one sanctification, and one God are the bases for this solidarity. Sin causes disunity and friction, and one of the gravest sins is the abuse of the tongue, so Paul reminded his readers that futile discourse (to say nothing of corrupt discourse) grieves the Holy Spirit (Eph. 4;29-31). The Spirit's presence in our lives ought to set a gatekeeper over our tongues.

The hostile weapon in the believer's defensive layer are the Sword of the Spirit and Prayer to God in the Spirit (Eph. 6:17, 18). The best approach to profound power is to be loaded with the Spirit, which essentially intends to be controlled by the Spirit (Eph. 5:18). The Holy Spirit in the believer's life and in the corporate of the congregation is clearly a main topic of this roundabout letter we call Ephesians.

The answer for the issues of the congregation today lies in tackling the issue of personal Christians, and cure is a person, the Holy Spirit.

He is cure for each blunder, the force for each shortcoming, the triumph for each thrashing, the supply for each need, and the response for each inquiry. He is accessible to each believer, for He lives in every believer's heart and life. The answers and power have as of now been given to us in the person of the Spirit who hotel each of us (Ryrie, 1955, 1997).

In the event that this were a book that offered you some new, supernatural, or mystery equation for profound power, I am certain the offers of it would be sensational. You would presumably eat up its substance at one sitting. This is not that sort of book, be that as it may, for these is no new and startling equation for profound power. There can be only the same old thing new or more to be added to what God has as of now given in the person of His Holy Spirit who lives in us. He is accessible as water; there is no requirement for extra costly pills, recipes, "insider facts," or projects.'

In any case, the compassion is that most Christians go about as I did at one time. We search for the new, the "inexplicable," the ensured equation, the most recent workshop, and we totally neglect the water that is uninhibitedly accessible. We rush to the evangelist or class leader who has some new mystery for triumph, and we overlook the Holy Spirit who has been unreservedly given to us and who needs to flood our lives. We don't need a greater amount of Him, yet we do frantically need to know a greater amount of Him, and with the expanded information will come included faith, power, and control in our lives. To learn requires some serious energy. Not just then, is there no recipe; there is no moment spiritual development and power.

I trust this investigation of the Spirit will help you to take in more of Him and result in complete yieldedness to His control, and full experience of His numerous services, to the end that the living Lord Jesus Christ will show in your life. When this is done, then we can realize that we have adapted well the regulation of the Holy Spirit" (Ryrie, 1965, 1997). You Can Believe This!

Related To Believers

The Holy Spirit is related to the reasoning of believers. At the Council of Jerusalem the pupils announced, "It appeared to be great to us and to the Holy Spirit" (Acts 15:28).

The Holy Spirit is not just a man – He is Deity (God). He is particularly called "God" in the Ananias occurrence (Acts 5:4).

Paul says, "Now the lord is the Spirit" (II Cor. 3:17); cf. 19), and once more, "Don't you know you yourselves are God's people…that God's Spirit abides in you?" (I Cor. 3:16).

Our Lord says that obscenity against the Holy Spirit is more awful than profanation against the Son of man. This must imply that impiety against the Spirit defames and dishonors God.

The Holy Spirit have ascribes which have a place only to deity. He is interminable: "Christ, who through the unceasing Spirit offered Himself" (Heb. 9:14). He is ubiquitous: "Where would I be able to go from the Spirit" Where would I be able to escape from your presence?" (Ps, 139:7). He is the Spirit of Life (Rom. 8:2) and the Spirit of Truth (Jn. 16:13).

The Holy Spirit does God's work. He was included in creation" "The Spirit of God moved upon the … waters" (Gen. 1:2). He is included in recovery, the new birth: "So it is with everybody born of the Spirit" (Jn. 3:8). Jesus Christ cast out devils by the Spirit of God (Matt. 12:28). The Holy Spirit partakes in resurrection: "And if the Spirit of him who raised Jesus from the dead is living in You, He... will likewise offer life to your mortal bodies through His Spirit, who lives in you" (Rom. 8:11).

The New Testament cites numerous Old Testament entries in which the speaker is Jehovah, the Lord. In the New Testament, such messages are regularly ascribed to the Holy Spirit. Isaiah said, "I heard the voice of the Lord" (Isa. 6:8). In any case, Paul said, "The Holy Spirit talked truth to your ancestors when He said through Isaiah the prophet..." You will be regularly hearing, yet never understanding" (Acts 28:25, 26).

Generally as reality of the "Trinity" is implied in the Old Testament yet anticipates its fullest expression in the New Testament, so with 'truth" about the Holy Spirit. His identity and deity are clear in the Old Testament, yet the full articulation of His action is given in the New Testament. There is no contention here with the Old Testament, yet the New Testament picture is significantly more complete.

The Holy Spirit's Part In Creation

The work of creation is for the most part credited to God without recognizing what specific parts of creation every person of the "Trinity" or "Godhead" may have been included in. Plainly, notwithstanding, all were included: God (Genesis 1-2), Christ (John 1:3), and the Holy Spirit.

From The Scriptures

Genesis 1:2. The work of the Spirit in creation is not explicitly said until after the creation (expecting what v. 1 records the truth of the first things God used as a part of creation and v. 2 starts the record of the designing of the world). Obviously as a person from the Trinity He took part in the demonstration of unique creation in 1:1. Particularly in verse 2, the Spirit "was moving over the surface of the waters."

The Hebrew word for "was moving" is used somewhere else as a part of the Old Testament only in Deuteronomy 32:11, where it is interpreted "floats," and in Jeremiah 23:9, where it is deciphered "tremble" or "shake." Apparently, the Spirit drifted over and looked after the first yet far unfashioned earth.

Psalm 33:6. Here the word interpreted "breath" is, obviously, the Hebrew word "spirit." Whether this is a reference to the Holy Spirit, be that as it may, it is begging to be proven wrong, for the "spirit of his mouth" can not be said to plainly allude to a man, to say nothing of unmistakably alluding to the third person of the Trinity. A few, by and by, do comprehend it as a kind of perspective to the Holy Spirit.

Psalm 104:30. This is by all accounts a clearer reference to the Holy Spirit, in spite of the fact that He can't emphatically be identified with the creative work recorded in Genesis 1-2. The reference to ocean creatures in verse 26 and the use in the Hebrew of the term "bara" (some of the time interpreted "made") in verse 30 may interface this to the Genesis creation. In these verses the Spirit is straightforwardly associated with the arranging and administration of the universe. These verses allude to the Spirit's work in making man.

From The Use Of Elohim

Despite the fact the structure Elohim is a veritable plural, it is without a doubt a plural of loftiness as opposed to a numerical plural; that is, it talks about God as the incomparable One, not of the Trinity. It connotes God, it is for the most part used with different parts of discourse in the solitary.

In spite of the fact that the word "Elohim" does not educate the Trinity of the Godhead, it allows for full and clear disclosure of the Trinity of God in the New Testament. In this manner, in the light of New Testament truth concerning the Trinity, the numerous references in Genesis 1 that allude to Elohim as the maker incorporate the work of the Son and of the Spirit alongside that of the Father.

In this manner Elohim in the light of New Testament disclosure is an additional confirmation of the way that the Holy Spirit shared the work of creation.

A Few Particulars of The Holy Spirit's Part In Creation

He Gave Life To The Creation

This is the fundamental work of the Holy Spirit in numerous territories, including that of "creation" (see John 6:63; II Cor. 3:6) He offers life to the creation (Job 27:3; 33:4; Psalm 104:30).

He Gave Order To The Creation

The creation is one of request. This is seen motel the waters, the heavens (sky), and the earth (Is. 40:12), and especially in the efficient procedure in the heaven (Job 26:13).

He Adorned The Creation

It was the Holy Spirit's specific work to enhance the creation to the eminence of God (Job 26:13; Psalm 33:6). The sky do pronounce the magnificence, the glory of God, and it appears as though this was one of the exceptional services of the Holy Spirit in connection to the work of creation.

He Preserves The Creation

In spite of the fact that Christ is typically connected with the conservation of the universe (Heb. 1:3), there is no less than one reference to the Holy Spirit's part in this work. Psalm 104:29-30 demonstrates the Spirit's part in making as well as His work of restoring, with the goal that it is safeguarded.

To Sum Up: Although not an incredible arrangement is said particularly in regards to the Holy Spirit's movement in creation, He was included. In this manner, as we ponder every one of the marvels of creation we owe in the presence of the One (Father, Son, And Holy Spirit) who finished this powerful accomplishment.

Yet, we likewise consider even a more noteworthy deed – the new creation which the Holy Spirit finishes through the new birth (Ryie, 1965, 1997).

A Divine Person

We should never refer to the "Holy Spirit" as "it," and we likewise, do not refer to the "Holy Spirit" as merely an "influence.' The

Holy Spirit is a divine person, known to be the third person of the "Trinity" or "Godhead.' The Trinity consists of two other persons known as God the Father and God the Son. Many refer to the third person of the Trinity or Godhead as God the Holy Spirit. However, He is known by other names such as: The Holy Ghost, The Spirit of Christ, The Spirit of God, and The Spirit of Truth.

In the Old Testament, the Holy Spirit is the originator and author of creation. The Bible declares in Genesis chapter One; "The earth was without form, void; and a darkness was upon the face of the deep.' "And the Spirit of God (Holy Spirit) moved upon the face of the waters."

The Spirit of God brought order out of chaos when He brooded over the earth. His Holy Spirit brought forth every living thing including mankind, the highest climax of all His creative acts. Unlike all other species of the animal kingdom, He created man with a soul and in His own likeness. The Spirit of God purposed day and night. He made dry land and seas separate; plants and trees, the sun, moon, stars, sea-life, birds and all manner of land mammals, creatures, and man (See Genesis 1; 2:1-7).

It was the Holy Spirit of God who inspired holy men to write the scriptures (II Pet. 1:21; II Tim. 3:16; Dan. 10:21; Acts 1:16); men such as Moses who wrote the first five books in the Bible known as the Pentateuch or the Book of Moses. The Holy Spirit of God inspired David to compose the Psalms; Solomon was inspired to write the Proverbs, Ecclesiastes and the Song Of Solomon. Isaiah, Daniel, and Jeremiah are accredited with many of the Old Testament prophecies along with many other Old Testament prophets who were likewise inspired by the Holy Spirit of God.

Great men such as Paul, Silas, and Barnabas were led by the Holy Spirit of God to travel missionary journeys found within the New Testament. The Holy Spirit revealed unto John on the "Isle of Patmos" some of heaven's closest secrets which John penned during his exile. These are a few found throughout the Book of Revelation concerning the Kingdom of Heaven and the Coming of the Messiah.

The Power of the Holy Spirit of God overshadowed the Virgin Mary and purposed, manifested the birth of Jesus Christ (See Luke 1:35). At Jesus Chirst's Baptism, found in Matthew 3;16-17, we read: "This is my beloved Son, in whom I am well pleased, and the Holy Spirit of God was seen descending like a dove, and lighting upon him." Only God can do these things aforementioned, He is God, The Holy Spirit.

The Holy Spirit Can Be
Lied To And Grieved

A lie may be expressed as communicating to one a sense of, or an impression of that which is false or untrue. To grieve the Holy Spirit means offending, deceiving, or resisting the Holy Spirit. Sin is what grieves the Holy Spirit. The only remedy for sins committed against the Holy Spirit is confession and repentance (see John 1:9; Matthew 3:2; Luke 15:7; Romans 2:4; Eph. 4:30).

The two terms "lie" and "grieve" may be expressed in action or spoken communication which reveals our attitude toward the Holy Spirit. So, we conclude that the Holy Spirit can be "lied" to (Acts 5:3) and the Holy Spirit can be "grieved" (Eph. 4:30).

In Acts 5:3, Peter is speaking to Ananias. He asks Ananias, "Ananias, why hath Satan (the devil) filled thine heart to lie to the Holy Ghost (Holy Spirit)?" The Wycliff Bible Commentary interprets as: "Peter charged Ananias not with deceiving him (Peter) but with attempting to deceive the Holy Spirit,"

"The program of sharing wealth in the early church was a purely voluntary one and not compulsory."

"While the land remained in Ananias' possession, it was his alone to dispose of as he chose; and even after he had sold it, the money was his to do with as he pleased.' "Ananias' sin did not consist of his keeping back the money, but in his pretending a complete consecration to God while deliberately keeping back part of the money.' "This was the sin of insincere consecration;" for it meant lying to God (God The Holy Spirit).

The Baptism With The Holy Spirit

Whosoever will accept the Lord Jesus Christ into their life as their Lord and Saviour is saved; and is baptized with His Holy Spirit at conversion. One is under the cleansing power of the blood of Jesus Christ our Lord who sends His Holy Spirit (Another Comforter) to dwell in the believer (John 3:3-8; Romans 10:9,10; 8:9).

The believer is set aside or set apart from the world (the believer is in the world, but not of the world). This is because the Holy Spirit brings one from a state of lostness to a state of salvation in Jesus Christ. The Old man is pulled off and the New man is put on. A New man or a New woman comes forth saved, sanctified, in righteousness, a new creation in Jesus Christ. Eph. 4:24 says: "And that ye put on the new man, which after God is created in righteousness and true holiness.'

It is the power of the Holy Spirit who converts, transforms from the old man (lost and unsaved) to the new man (saved, born again, a Christian). The Holy Spirit cleanses us from sin and gives us the power to be sons (and daughters) of God as we grow in grace.

John 1:12-14 says: "But as many as received him, to them gave he power to become sons of God, even to them that believe on his name: which were born, not of blood, nor of the will of the flesh, nor of the will of man, but of God. And the Word was made flesh, and dwelt among us (And we beheld his glory, the glory as of the only begotten of the Father), full of grace and truth." (See also Hebrews 10:16-23).

The Anointing With The Holy Spirit

At Conversion, the Holy Spirit regenerates, saves, transforms, and sanctifies us with the baptism of the Holy Spirit. The Anointing With the Holy Spirit also takes place at conversion (when we have accepted Jesus Christ as our Lord and Saviour). He anoints us with His power. The anointing is so called the in wrought power of the Holy Spirit whereby He empowers us to do the work of Jesus Christ. This is the Holy Spirit's dwelling in us, empowering us not only for the work Jesus Christ did; but He empowers us to live holy lives with Jesus Christ as our example.

Today, it is the powerful anointing of the Holy Spirit who gives us power to do the great tasks wherever the Lord Jesus has need of us to carry out His great work. The Holy Spirit is ever-present with us to sanction His authority and to supply the needed power for the satisfactory completion of every appointed holy task (See Lk. 3;21-22; John 14:17; Ephesians 1:13; Acts 10:38; Psalm 51:11-13).

The Sealing Ministry Of The Holy Spirit

(Sealed With The Holy Spirit)

The Sealing Ministry of the Holy Spirit means God has given His seal of approval to the new life in Jesus Christ, the service, and work of the anointed believer. The seal suggests possession, in that the believer belongs to God, and security in that the believer is promised salvation. Jesus Christ purchased us for Himself and gave us the Holy Spirit as the promise that our salvation would be complete.

I once heard a scholar state it in terms of ownership: "He owns me and has made me His own child by his own power." I know all the Holy Spirit has promised will come to pass because He has promised, guaranteed, sealed it up forever.' In other words, our salvation is sealed unto the day of redemption, as is the great work of salvation we render in the service we give to others as we are led by the Holy Spirit.

We are kept by the power of the Holy Spirit's "Sealing." Salvation is assured because Jesus Christ saved us by His Holy Spirit. The Holy Spirit lives in us, helping us to live according to the teachings of Jesus Christ (God's Word) and His example.

The Holy Spirit Bears
Witness Of The Truth

"When the Comforter is come, whom I will send unto you from the Father, ever the Spirit Of Truth, which proceedeth from the Father, He shall testify of me: and ye also shall bear witness, because ye have been with me from the beginning' (John 15:26-27).

The Holy Spirit Is Helper, Counselor And
Advocate Who Teaches And Reminds

"These things have I spoken unto you, being yet present with you. But the Comforter, which is the Holy Ghost, whom the Father will send in my name, he shall teach you all things, and bring all things to your remembrance, whatsoever I have said unto you" (John 14:25-26).

Symbols Of The Holy Spirit

"Dove'

The dove represents the peaceful gentleness of the work and operation of the Holy Spirit. Matthew 10:16 says: "Behold, I send you forth as sheep in the midst of wolves: be ye therefore, wise as serpents, and harmless as doves." John said, "I saw the Spirit descending from heaven like a dove, and it abode upon him" (John 1:32).

The "dove" represents the Spirit of Truth as indicated in John 14:17. "Even the Spirit of Truth; whom the world cannot receive, because it seeth him not, neither knoweth him: but ye know him; for he dwelleth with you, and shall be in you."

The dove is the Spirit of Light who makes all things clear to us as found in Ephesians 1:17 and reads: "That the God of Our Lord Jesus Christ, the Father of glory, may give unto you the spirit of wisdom and revelation in the knowledge of him."

"Water"

Water represents an abundance of the Spirit. Jesus Christ said: "Whosoever drinketh of this water shall never thirst again: But whosoever drinketh of the water that I shall give him shall never thirst; the water that I shall give him shall be in him a well of water springing up into everlasting life" (John 4:13,14).

You Can Believe This!

"Fire"

It may be said that "fire" represents the purifying, cleansing, quickening, motivating influence of the Holy Spirit within the life of the believer. The believer is on fire for Our Lord Jesus Christ. He (The Holy Spirit) starts the fire in us, stirs up the fire, then spreads the fire. Hebrews 1:7 says: "And of the angels he saith, Who maketh his angels spirits, and his ministers a flame of fire.' A fire which empowers (Acts 1:5-8).

In II Thess. 1:8 we read: "In a flaming fire taking vengeance on them that know not God, and that obey not the gospel of Our Lord Jesus Christ."

It may well be noted that fire may be symbolic of a fire which tries and proves which is called "A Consuming Fire.' Hebrews 12:28, 29 says: "Wherefore we receiving a kingdom which cannot be moved, let us have grace, whereby we may serve God acceptably with reverence and godly fear: For Our God is a consuming fire."

"Oil"

In the Old Testament, Oil was used to anoint priests (Exodus 29:7) and kings (I Samuel 12:3-5). Jesus said: "The Spirit of the Lord is upon me, because he hath anointed me to preach the gospel (Luke 4:18)." Paul said in II Corinthians 1:21, 22: "He which establisheth us with you in Christ, and hath anointed us, is God, who hath also sealed us, and given the earnest of the Spirit in our hearts."

"Wind/Breath"

"Breath" represents the Holy Spirit in Genesis 2:7 which reads: "And the Lord God formed man of the dust of the ground, and breathed into his nostrils the "breath of life;"

and man became a living soul.' Acts 17:25 says: "Neither is worshiped with men's hands, as though he needed any thing, seeing he giveth to all life, and breath, and all things.'

In Genesis 12 we read: "And the Spirit of God moved upon the face of the waters.' Genesis 6:3 says: "My Spirit shall not always strive with man.' John 3:8 reads: "The wind bloweth where it listeth, and thou hearest the sound thereof, but canst not tell whence it cometh, and whither it goeth: so is every one that is born of the Spirit."

"Denied To Sinners"

"Cast me not away from my presence; and take not thy Holy Spirit from me" (Ps. 51:11). "Wherefore I say unto you, all manner of sin and blasphemy shall be forgiven unto men; but the blasphemy against the Holy Ghost shall not be forgiven unto men" (Matthew 12:31).

"Eternal"

"How much more shall the blood of Christ, who through the eternal Spirit offered himself without spot to God, purge your conscience from dead works to serve the living God" (Heb. 9:14).

Gifts Of The Holy Spirit

"Full Of Gifts"

"But if the Spirit of Him that raised up Jesus from the dead dwell in you, he that raised up Christ from the dead shall also quicken your mortal bodies by his Spirit that dwelleth in you" (Romans 8:11).

"But the fruit of the Spirit is love, joy, peace, long suffering, gentleness, goodness, faith, meekness, temperance: against such there is no law" (Galatians 5:22, 23).

Inspires God's Word

"Men and brethren, this Scripture must needs have been fulfilled, which the Holy Ghost by the mouth of David spake before concerning Judas, which was guide to them that took Jesus" (Acts 1:16).

"Knowing this first, that no prophecy of the Scripture is of any private interpretation, for the prophecy came not in old time by the will of man; but holy men of God spake as they were moved by the Holy Ghost" (II Peter 1:20-21).

"Ministers To Us"

"Howbeit when he, the Spirit of Truth, is come, he will guide you into all truth; for he shall not speak of himself; but whatsoever he shall hear, that he shall speak: and he will shew you things to come" (John 16:13).

"But God hath revealed them unto us by his Spirit: for the Spirit searcheth all things, yea. The deep things of God" (I Cor. 2:10).

"Pours Out His Spirit"

"And it shall come to pass afterward, that I will pour out my Spirit upon all flesh; and your sons and your daughters shall prophecy, your old men shall dream dreams, your young men shall see visions" (Joel 2:28).

"But ye shall receive power, after that the Holy Ghost is come upon you: and ye shall be witness unto me both in Jerusalem, and in all Judea, and in Samaria, and unto the uttermost part of the earth" (Acts 1:8).

"The Holy Spirit Is The Quickner Of The Spirit"

"But if the Spirit of him that raised up Jesus from the dead dwell in you, he that raised up Christ from the dead shall also quicken your mortal bodies by his Spirit that dwelleth in you" (Romans 8:11).

"The Holy Spirit Is A Teacher"

"And it was revealed unto him by the Holy Ghost, that he should not see death, before he had seen the Lord's Christ" (Luke 2:26).

"Howbeit when he, the Spirit of Truth, is come, he will guide you into all truth: for he shall not speak of himself; but whatsoever he shall hear, that shall he speak; and he will show you things to come" (John 16:13).

"The Holy Spirit Is The Spirit Of Truth"

"Even the Spirit of Truth; whom the world cannot receive, because it seeth him not, neither knoweth him: but ye know him; for he dwelleth with you, and shall be in you" (John 14:17).

"But when the Comforter is come, when I will send you from the Father, even the Spirit of Truth, which proceedeth from the Father, he shall testify of me" (John 15:26).

"We are of God: he that knoweth God heareth us; he that is not of God heareth not us. Hereby know ye the Spirit of Truth, and the spirit of error" (I John 4:6).

The Holy Spirit Is Not To Be Sinned Against

"And grieve not the Holy Spirit of God, whereby ye are sealed unto the day of redemption" (Eph. 4:30).

"But they rebelled, and vexed his Holy Spirit; therefore he was turned to be their enemy, and he fought against them" (Is. 63:10).

"Wherefore I say unto you, all manner of sin and blasphemy shall be forgiven unto men: but the blasphemy against the Holy Ghost shall not be forgiven unto men" (Matt. 12:31).

"And whosoever speaketh a word against the Son of man, it shall be forgiven him: but whosoever speaketh against the Holy Ghost, it shall not be forgiven him, neither in this world, neither in the world to come" (Matt. 12:32).

CHAPTER

NINE

Gifts Granted By The Holy Spirit To The Believer

There are gifts which the Holy Spirit indwells, imparts within the child of God. No two gifts are exactly the same within the community of believers. The Holy Spirit grants unto us the several gifts for the work of the ministry, for edifying the body of Jesus Christ, for the common good, for the perfecting of the saints, employed in serving one another as good stewards of the manifold grace of God.

Jesus said: "The Spirit of the Lord is upon me, because he hath anointed me to preach the gospel to the poor; He hath sent me to heal the broken-hearted, to preach deliverance to the captives, and recovering of sight to the blind, to set at liberty them that are bruised, To Preach the acceptable year of the Lord" (Luke 4:18, 19).

The Holy Spirit bestows gifts upon the believer as an endowment of useful service. No believer should feel his gift is superior to others, but to serve the Christian church. The Holy Spirit has rendered unto us gifts in order that we might render better service to one another and others in love glorifying Jesus Christ.

Romans 12:3 reads" "For I say, through the grace given unto me, to every man that is among you, not to think more highly than he ought to think; but to think soberly, according to God who hath dealt to every man the measure of faith."

Romans 12:4-8 reads: "For as many members in one body, and all members have not the same office: So we, being many, are one body in Christ, and every one member one of another." "Having then gifts differing according to the grace that is given to us, whether prophecy, let us prophesy according to the proportion of faith; Or ministry, let us wait on our ministering: or he that teacheth, on teaching; Or he that exhorteth, on exhortation: he that giveth, let him do it with simplicity; he that ruleth, with diligence; he that sheweth mercy, with cheerfulness."

The Bible declares: "And there are diversities of operations, but it is the same God which worketh all in all. But the manifestation of the Spirit is given to every man to profit withal. For to one is given by the Spirit the word of wisdom; to another the word of knowledge by the same Spirit; to another faith by the same Spirit; to another the gift of healing by the same Spirit;

to another the working of miracles; to another prophecy; to another discerning of spirits; to another diverse kinds of tongues: But all these worketh that one and the self same Spirit, dividing to every man severally as he will" (I Cor. 1`2:6-11).

"And God hath set some in the church, first apostles, secondarily prophets, thirdly teachers, after that miracles, then gifts of healing, helps, governments, diversities of tongues. Are all apostles? Are all prophets? Are all teachers? Are all workers of miracles? Have all the gifts healing? Do all speak with tongues? Do all interpret?" (I Cor. 12:28-30).

"But unto every one of us is given grace according to the measure of the gift of Christ," "And he gave some apostles, and some, prophets; and some evangelists;

and some, pastors and teachers; For the perfecting of the saints, for the work of the ministry, for the edifying of the body of Christ: Till we all come in unity of faith, and of the knowledge of the Son of God, unto a perfect man, unto the measure of the stature of the fullness of Christ: That we henceforth be no more children, tossed to and fro, and carried about with every wind of doctrine, by the slight of man, and cunning craftiness, whereby they lie in wait to deceive, But speaking the truth in love, may grow up into him in all things, which is the head, even Christ; From whom the whole body fitly joined together and compacted by that which every joint supplieth, according to the effectual working in the measure of the body unto the edifying of itself in love" (Ephesians 4:7,11-16).

Gifts Of The Holy Spirit

Apostles – The title of the twelve disciples (Matt. 10:2; Mark 6:30; Luke 6:13). one Sent. The term was used of Christ (Heb. 3;1); and also denoted any commissioned to preach the gospel (II Cor. 8:23; Phil. 2:25). It was Paul's self-designation (Rom. 1:1).

Prophet – One qualified by God to make announcement in inspired words. He was therefore quite as much the spokesman for God, as he was one who spoke before an event happened and anticipated its occurrence (In the Old Testament was called the Nabi; seer; I Sam. 9:9; II Sam. 24:11; I Chr. 9:22). A translation of two Hebrew words which mean to gaze intently and thus to so carefully observe the past and present as to be able to discount the future with assurance.

Pastors And Teachers – Ministers who lead, guide, feed, guard, oversee, teach the flock (Jer. 17:16; Eph. 4:11; I Tim. 2:7; Jer. 3;15; I Thess. 3:2).

Evangelist – one who preaches the Gospel and is distinct from apostles, prophets, pastors, and teachers (Eph. 4;11; Acts 21:8; II Tim. 4;5).

Prophecy – To exhort, encourage, and comfort in correct relationship to the revealed Word of God (Truth of God) (I Cor. 14:3); a message, predict (Neh. 6:12); gift of prophecy (I Cor. 13:2).

Teaching – To teach or to instruct (II Tim. 2:2; Ps. 27:11; Jer. 32:23).

Exhortation – And appeal; encouragement (Acts 13:15; I Cor. 14:3; Heb. 3:13; I Tim. 4:13).

Giving – Should be done with cheerfulness, liberality (II Cor. 9:7), give glory to God (Rom. 4:20; Mal. 2:2).

Ruling – To aid, to lead (I Chr. 9:11; II Sam. 6:21; I Sam. 25:30; Matt 24:45). (kings, stewards, high priests, elders; see elders (I Tim. 5:17).

Showing Mercy – Showing kindness (Ps. 6:4; Ps. 23:6; Mic. 6:8; Eph. 2:4; I Tim. 1:2; Heb. 4:16).

Word of Wisdom – Communication of spiritual wisdom (James 1:5), as contained in the Epistles. Necessary in early days when the church possessed no New Testament.

Word of Knowledge – Had to do with truth or a more practical character (the practical sections of the Epistles): It too, was possibly a temporary gift.

The Word of God is sufficient now (I Cor. 12:6-10).

Miracles – A remarkable happening beyond or contrary to the laws of nature, performed through divine power (Matt. 12:28; John 3:2; Rom. 15:19).

Healing – Power to heal is from God (Ex. 15:26; Ps. 103:3; 147:3). It was abundantly evident in Jesus (Matt. 8:5-16; Mark 7:24-30; Luke 14:1-6; John 4:46-54) Who gave this power to his disciples (Matt. 10:1-8; Luke 9:2). Used by Peter (Acts 3:6-8) and by Paul (Acts 20:9, 10).

Discerning Spirits – Is done by the Spirit through the Word (I Cor, 12:6-10).

Faith – Faith that performs miracles; faith that is steadfast, with confidence and conviction; faith that expresses itself through works of love and obedience (James 2:17; I Cor. 12:9; Gal. 3:26, 27; Rom. 3:25; Heb. 11- 12:2).

Tongues – There should always be a translator present when tongues are spoken, an interpreter. Tongues are not evidence of salvation, but love. One is not lost because he does not speak in tongues (see I Cor. 12 through I Cor. 14 in its entirety). If there is no translator or interpreter present to interpret tongues which may be spoken, then the one speaking tongues should cease, remain silent) (if one refuses to be silent when there is no interpreter then they are out of order).

Helps – Care for church finances, support of the ministry, relief of the poor and needy, aids, assisting in Christian service and worship services, and, perhaps, a host of other aids in helping the church.

The Holy Spirit commands, teaches, instructs (Acts 1). He leads and guides us into all truth. The Holy Spirit represents Jesus Christ and lives eternally with us (Rom. 5:5; Luke 2:26; 12:12; Matthew 1:18, 20; 3:11; 28:19; Mark 1:8,

24; 13:11; Luke 1:35, 41, 49; John 14:26; Acts 1:8; Acts 2:4; 4:8).

Who Is The Holy Spirit? He is God's presence in the Human Heart!

CHAPTER
TEN

The Trinity

(The Godhead)

When we say God the Creator, Christ Our Redeemer, and The Holy Spirit Our Comforter; we ought to clearly see God the Father, God the Son and God the Holy Spirit. Not three individual persons, but three persons in one. The Trinity or Godhead is God the Father who created us, God the Son who redeems us, and God the Holy Spirit who comforts us, empowers us and deal with us.

The concept or doctrine of the Trinity is one which has been misunderstood because many person think in terms of three individual persons or separate persons. There are not three separate persons but Only One God who acts and reveals Himself as God the Father, God the Son, and God the Holy Spirit. This is the mystery of the Godhead.

We can not do proper justice to the concept or doctrine of the trinity on the human level. We can only understand on the spiritual level (and only God The Holy Spirit can reveal that to us).

We can accept it or we can reject it as many do; but God will still be God the Father, God the Son and God the Holy Spirit. Acts 17:29 reads: 'Forasmuch then as we are the offspring of God, we ought not to think that the Godhead is like unto gold, or silver, or stone, graven by art and man's device. "For the invisible things of him (God) from the creation of the world are clearly seen, being understood by the things that are made, even his eternal power and Godhead; so that they are without excuse" (Romans 1:20).

'For in him dwelleth all the fullness of the Godhead bodily" (Col. 1:8). Jesus said: "But the comforter, which is the Holy Ghosty, whom the Father will send in my name, he shall teach you all things, and bring all things to your remembrance, whatsoever I have said unto you" (John 14:260. In I John 5:7 we read: "For there are three that bear record in heaven, the Father, the Word, and the Holy Ghost: and these three are one.'

God The Father

"One Lord, one faith, one baptism, One God and Father of all, who is above all, and through all, and in you all" (Eph. 4:5, 6).

"At that time Jesus answered and said, I thank thee, O Father, Lord of heaven and earth, because thou hast hid these things from the wise and prudent, and hast revealed them unto babes" (Matt. 11:25).

"Labour not for the meat which perisheth, but for that meat which endureth unto everlasting life, which the Son of man shall give unto you: for him hath God the Father sealed" (John 6:27).

God The Son

"...This is my beloved Son, in whom I am well pleased" (Matt. 3:16, 17; Mark 1:10, 11; Luke 3:21, 22).

"In the beginning was the Word, and the Word was with God, and the Word was God, the same was in the beginning with God" (John 1:1).

"He that hath seen me hath seen the Father" (John 14:9).

God The Holy Spirit

"But God hath revealed them unto us by his Spirit: for the Spirit searcheth all things, yea, the deep things of God" (I Cor. 2:10).

In Summary

In the simplest possible words we may say the Trinity (GodHead) means that God is the Father, God is the Son, and God is the Holy Spirit (Three Manifestations of the person of God). There are not three separate persons, but three persons in one (a spiritual mystery, one of the deep things of God0. God reveals himself as Father, Son, and Holy Spirit. "For there are three that bear record in heaven, the Father, The Word, (or The Son), and The Holy Spirit: and these three are but the One True and Living God. (I John 5:6).

Although the term "Trinity" is not found within the pages of the Bible, the doctrine or concept of the Godhead is indicated within the Scriptures as follows: Genesis 3:22; 11:7; Isaiah 48:16; 61:1-3; Matthew 12:28; 28:19; Luke 1:35; 3:22; John 1:32; 14:16, 17, 26; Galatians 4:6; I John 5:6; Acts 17:19; Romans 1:20; I John 5:7; John 14:9; I Corinthians 2:10.

CHAPTER

ELEVEN

There Is A Devil!

Ye are of your father, the devil, and the lusts of your father ye will do. He was a murderer from the beginning, and abode not in the truth, because there is no truth in him – (John 8:44).

He that committeth sin is of the devil; for the devil sinneth from the beginning. For this purpose the Son of God was manifested, that he might destroy the works of the` devil – (I John 34:8).

The Bible discloses to us next to no source of the devil. It seems to derive that he was at one time a lead celestial host, a chief heavenly messenger, an archangel of awesome power and grandness. On account of this high position, and drove on by this pomposity, he turned out to be proud to the point that God needed to cast him out of heaven.

Presently he is allowed to go about on the earth tempting individuals and going about as a forceful foe. This musing is for the most part acknowledged by Bible researchers today. God made everything good, except a portion of his creations turned out to be terrible - man, for instance. It is sensible to trust that the fallen angel was made in goodness, however that he ended up malicious and was then cast out of heaven.

He is called by various names - Satan, Beelzebub, the evil one, the serpent, the dragon, the prince of this world and the ruler of this world. It doesn't make a difference what we call him - he is the devil!

There Is A Devil!

Numerous individuals say that the fallen angel, the devil doesn't exist, that he is just a fabrication of the creative ability. Christian Scientists say "all is great." But any sensible person realizes that everything is bad, and that there is a strong being behind all malevolent, to be specific, the devil.

The Bible Proves His Existence

Jesus Christ said in John 8:44, "The devil is." in Matthew 13:19, where Jesus was clarifying the story of the sower, he stated, "The evil on..., catcheth away that which was sown in his heart.'

If we say there is no devil, we make Jesus a liar. Peter said that there is a devil - John and Paul let us know of his reality. In any case, Jesus' words are sufficient for us. To prevent the presence from claiming the evil one is to deny the honesty and reliability of Jesus Chirst. We realize that the villain showed up upon the earth. We see him seeming to Job. He appeared to Jesus in the great temptation and at different occasions. He is appeared in the book of Revelation as seeming commonly upon the earth.

Experience Attests That There Is A Devil

We know from human experience that Satan is on the earth and on his job. There is a drive and a longing in each on of us to take after sinful ways, evil. Does this motivation originate from God? No! It originates from the devil. It originates from a source outside God, regardless of what name we provide for that source, we know it as the devil.

Each Christian in this world has a consistent battle against the powers of evil. He is enticed on each side. These allurements come in some cases notwithstanding when the offspring of God is in the blessed place of prayer. The devil brings this abhorrence into our minds. Each one of us is faced each day with the influence and power of a personal devil.

CHAPTER

TWELVE

He Is A Person

I John 3:8 says, "The devil sinneth." We all know only a man can be said to sin. This doesn't really imply that he has a body as we have, however he is a man in any case. He knows, he believes, he wills. The sketch artists generally picture the fiend similar to a red figure with a long tail and a pitchfork. He doesn't show up in that frame. If he came in that shape, we would know him and keep away from him. Be that as it may, when he comes to tempt us, he regularly comes in beauty and advances to us in the most alluring way.

We require a defensive layer against the devil. We discover this defensive layer in Ephesians 6:11-12, which peruses as takes after: """Put on the whole armour of God, that ye may be able to stand against the wiles of the devil. For we wrestle not against flesh and blood, but against principalities, against powers, against the rulers of the darkness of this world, against spiritual wickedness in high places."

We are battling against a real individual person. Jesus Christ and the entire Bible show us that he is a man. An arrangement of precept without an individual villain is a framework which is drastically unchristian and unscriptural.

The Devil Is A Being Of Great Power And Authority

Satan is a strong personality, and we can not battle only him. We require all the assistance of paradise in our battle against the devil. Think about the numerous contentions over our reality in a clash of the spirits of men and this compelling individual being whom we know as Satan. Think about all the wrongdoing (sins), the murders, the wars, the distresses, sins and a large group of different inconveniences on the planet.

What does everything extremely mean? It is basically a piece of the immense clash amongst great and shrewdness, between the spiritual good powers and evil powers.

We should disparage. We can't dismiss him. The enormous battle is on in our souls and in this world. Satan is fighting against God and his children and everything good that exists. Then again, we should not overestimate the devil.

We can not stand to get blue about it and say, "The world is going to the devil." We are in a fight, however He who is for us is more noteworthy than the person who battles against us. The devil is compelling, however the Savior is Almighty. We can defeat him through Jesus Christ. The fallen angel, the devil does numerous fiendish things, Butt God will defeat him in the end.

The Devil Is A Being Of Great Majesty And Dignity Of Position

Jude 9 reads: "Yet Michael the archangel, when contending with the devil he disputed about the body of Moses, durst not bring against him a railing accusation, but said, The Lord rebuke thee."

It appears that Michael, the lead celestial host of paradise, the archangel; squabbled with the devil over the body of Moses. We see that the situation of Satan was exalted to the point that even Michael did not set out bring a railing allegation against him, butt rather called upon the Lord to rebuke Satan.

In the event that a holy angel who possessed such a high position challenged not reproach Satan, without a doubt Satan's position more likely than not been a high one undoubtedly. Indeed, the devil is a person of awesome greatness, great majesty and dignity of position.

The Devil Is Prince Of This World

This is where we come in contact with him. If he were simply some great king or president thousands of miles away from us, we should never need to be concerned about him; but he is right here in this world carrying on his evil work, and we come in contact with the devil every day.

John 14:30: "Hereafter I will not talk much with you: for the prince of this world cometh, and hath nothing in me."

Look around you for a moment and you will see that the devil is ruling today as the prince of this world. We can never have permanent peace in this world, because he rules in the hearts and minds of the world's great leaders. The worldly man is out for personal gain; he has a greedy heart and seeks to gain everything and anything available. He does not respect the rights of others. How true this is of individuals as well as nations. The devil is ruling human hearts. Many conditions of war and hatred and greed prevail throughout many parts of our world today. There is only one answer to all these sorts of questions. The devil is ruling in the hearts of men all over the world. He has the upper hand in many lives. He sits upon the throne of many hearts. A boy is killed and missing over here and a small young woman is missing over there for years- a man and woman kill an aged person for their money. A woman takes the down hill trail to the road that leads to disgrace and ruin. All of this is because of sin.

The devil is behind every one of these things. He even enters the church and enters the hearts of some church members, causing them to do things which only the devil could think of. What a pitiful and tragic thing it is to let the devil rule in the heart in place of the Lord Jesus Christ!

CHAPTER

THIRTEEN

The Devil Is Wicked

God is the Holy One of heaven. He is the embodiment of perfect holiness. The devil is just the opposite. He is the embodiment of unholiness. Satan is the embodiment of consummate wickedness, evil. He is evil of the worst kind working his evil in the world.

The Devil Is The Original Sinner

First John 3:8 says: "He that committeth sin is of the devil; for the devil sinneth from the beginning. For this purpose the Son of God was manifested, that he might destroy the works of the devil (Sin, Evil)."

For what reason do men sin today? It is on the grounds that they have a place with the devil; they have his tendency in their flesh. Why, at that point, do Christians sin? They have been saved, however despite everything they hold their old corrupt natures. They never lose that nature until Jesus Christ in the twinkling of an eye changes them and makes them like unto himself.

The insidious (sinful nature) nature inside the Christian is continually battling against the good nature-the spiritual nature. The flesh of this world sins-the divine spirit inside a Christian repents. When I sin, my flesh has the rule of me. When I repent of that sin, my spirit is ruling me.

The devil tempts the Christian, and the Christian frequently falls into wrongdoing (sin). He can state, notwithstanding, with Paul, "It is no more I that do it, but the sin that dwelleth in me." The Christian who sins without a doubt is a pitiable man, but he can state again with Paul, "I thank God that through Jesus Christ our Lord I can be delivered from the body of this death."

The Work Of The Devil

The Devil Lies To Men

We are informed that the devil is the "father of lies." We can not confide in any person who tells lies, for the devil has concocted each lie at any point told. The devil misleads men today. He says to them, "Follow me into the pathways of transgression (sin) and I will give you the sweetness of life (a lie)." The devil is lying, since he can't do it. The devil can give you the joys of transgression for a season, however at last you drink the intense leftovers of dissatisfaction and depression as you sink down into unceasing damnation and hell.

Here is an old man, bowed, hopeless and dark. When he was a young fellow with all of life lying out before him. Be that as it may, the fallen angel (devil) deceived him. The devil enlightened him concerning the great things he could have in the event that he would take after the ways for transgression (sin) and the world.

The young fellow stated, "I will take everything in." He drank from each measure of sin, he tasted the sweetness of each wellspring of evildoing - he squandered his life years in crazy, riotous living.

Presently he has nothing left except for the severe recollections of a squandered existence without Jesus Christ. He has no delight in the present, he has no desire for what's to come. It has been well said that the devil has no happy old people.

The Devil Is The Author Of False Views

2nd Corinthians 4:4 says: "In whom the god of this world hath blinded the minds of them which believe not, lest the light of the glorious gospel of Christ, who is the image of God, should shine unto them."

Everywhere throughout the world the devil has possessed the power to make men question the old things which have been accepted down through the ages. The devil particularly brings questions concerning the person of Christ; he is always telling men that Christ isn't divine. He starts an insidious work by planting an uncertainty in our souls; at that point he is effectively ready to lead us endlessly into transgression (sin).

In the garden of Eden, when the devil enticed Eve, she said to him, "God has let us know not to eat of the fruit of this specific tree, saying that in the event that we do eat it we will surely die."

Then the fiend answered in an extremely mocking vein, "Ye will not surely die."

The seed was planted-the uncertainty, doubt started to develop and soon Eve had been cleared down into the guilt of wrongdoing (sin). He even attempted to bring question into Jesus' mind when he stated, "If thou be the Son of God."

The betting corridors, the alcohol joints, the places of ignominy are not by any means the only places of Satan's exercises. He is working in numerous schools and universities in the land. People are instructing youthful young men and young women to question the Word of God. They call the Bible "old fogy stuff" and urge the understudies to divert from mother's religion (Christianity).

The devil realizes that if he can make these youngsters question the Bible, he can before long lead them off into transgression (sin). I know it is valid, for I have seen it on numerous occasions.

Jesus Christ must be the focal point of our schools. Christ and the Word of God must be the focal point of our instructive life if Christianity is to flourish and if Christian pioneers are to be sent into this evil world.

CHAPTER

FOURTEEN

The Destiny Of The Devil

Revelation 20:10 says: "And the devil that deceived them was cast into the lake of fire and brimstone, where the beast and the false prophet are, and shall be tormented day and night for ever and ever."

At the point when the devil descends to his last end, his predetermination will be in the everlasting flames of damnation, hell. The devil won't be distant from everyone else - his followers will be with him. Hell is a "place prepared for the devil and his angels." It is a position of just and upright punishment. In the event that you go to hell, it will be on account of you joining up with the devil (Satan) instead of with God.

Everybody who rejects Jesus Christ is putting his support behind Satan, and there is nothing left for him except for everlasting hell.

How To Get Victory Over The Devil
Surrender To God And Resist The Devil

James 4:7 says: "Submit yourselves therefore to God. Resist the devil, and he will flee from you."

When we resist the devil in our own strength, we will dependably fall flat. In any case, the when we surrender to God, we have all his power on our side. The issue with the greater part of us is that we don't avoid the suggestions of Satan. When he entices us, we grasp the chance to sin; however in the event that we are to conquer Satan, we should resist him in the strength of the Lord.

We should say to him, "I can't yield to this thing because I am a child of God." Surely the Lord will encourage us if we assume such a disposition, and if in that way we beat the devil, we will be more grounded to defeat him the next time.

Store Up God's Word And God's Promises In Our Hearts

Jesus Christ defeated the devil by remembering and resting on the Word of God. We are to recall every one of the promises which he makes to those who stand up for him. When we disregard perusing and studying the Bible, we are leaving the windows totally open, and the devil can come in and conquer us.

God gives his strength through his Word, and we should stand upon that Word in the event that we are to be sufficiently strong enough to overcome the evil one, the devil.

Put On The Whole Armor Of God

We can hold the shield of faith before us by saying in our hearts, "This is the victory that overcometh the world, even our faith." We are to wear the helmet of salvation, shouting, "I am saved, I belong to Jesus Christ, and I won't respect this enticement (temptation)." We should wield the sword of the Spirit, using the Bible and its truth upon the devil and thus sending him back to his hot hole in hell.

We Are To Claim Jesus Christ's Strength For Ours

Ephesians 6:10: "Finally, my brethren, be strong in the Lord, and in the power of his might."

When temptations come and cry out, "Lord, help me," he will give us strength. He has never refused yet to help those who call upon him as they take part in their battles against the prince of this world.

A good Christian man lay dying. Calling his children to the bedside, he had a decent word for every one of them and after that kissed them farewell. At long last he swung to his significant other and said to her, "When I am gone, you will confide in the Lord and discover your solace in him, won't you?" And she replied, "Indeed, dear. "I know whom I have accepted, and am influenced that he can keep what I have submitted unto him against that day!"

Her significant other at that point stated: "You and I have been to the graveyard four times to secure those whom we loved, and you will recollect that each time as we rode back home God spoke his solace and effortlessness (grace) to us in each turn of the wheels.

Presently, when I am gone, I realize that you will swing to him for your solace in the hour of distress." The good man at that point started to cite the twenty-third Psalm, and when he came in to the refrain which says, "Though I walk through the valley of the shadow of death, I will fear no evil," he swung to his better half and stated, "Mary, he is with me now and I am going home with him."

He had lived with the overcoming life, and now he had gone out to meet his Savior and to get his reward.

The devil might control your heart since you do those things which you should not do. He might deny you of peace and power and solace.

Beloved, come to Jesus Christ every day, cast all your cares upon him, put your hand in the nail-punctured hand, and you, as well, will be able to live the "Victorious Life."

CHAPTER
FIFTEEN

The Gospel Church

The visible church is a body of baptized believers in Jesus Christ, the New Testament Church, associated by a covenant in Christian Faith. They have a fellowship in view of the Gospel standards making a Christian community. Every adult part has the privilege to vote and each vote means a single one. Each person is said to be guided all in all by the aid of the Holy Spirit.

There are two scriptural officers, pastors and deacons. All others are designated or elected as the need emerges. The officers are characterized in First Timothy and Titus.

The congregation has three different ways of receiving members, a candidate for baptism, Christian experience and by letter. The congregation also has three ways of dismissal: by death, by letter and by expulsion (dismissal).

We believe Jesus Christ gave the Church a definite place in the Kingdom program when He said to Peter, "I will give you the keys to the Kingdom and those you receive on earth will be received in heaven and those you reject on earth will be rejected in heaven."

The Gospel Church uses the Bible as their guide. The Gospel Church must serve all people and judge them not. Jesus Christ will be the Separator. The wheat and tares will grow together regardless of how cautious the farmer plants the seeds.

The Church belongs to God, not the community.

(Matthew 16:18; 18:17; Acts 2:47; 15:4; I Corinthians 4:17; 14:34; Revelation 2:23).

The Christian Sabbath

We believe that Sunday, the first day of the week, is the Lord's Day. Christians ought to remember it and keep it consecrated for religious purposes.

Having worship services on Saturday depended on the way that God labored for six days and on the seventh day He rested. We don't know that this word "rest" implies that God was tired (since God has no physical body to get worn out), yet one thing we do know is that man was not qualified for a rest on the seventh day since God made everything else on the initial five days and made man on the 6th day.

Along these lines, man would have been one day old on the day God rested (rest may suggest that God had completed all his wondrous acts of creation).

The idea of having worship on Saturday involved a covenant between God and the Jews. They worked under the Law (Judaism), we work under grace and love (Christianity). The churches that believe in monotheism or one God can observe Saturday or seventh day due to the promise that God made to Abraham. We commend the first day of the week as "Resurrection Day," The Christian Sabbath. (Mark 16:2-9; John 20:1; Exodus 12:18).

The Righteous And The Wicked

"He that believeth and is baptized shall be saved. He that believeth not shall be damned" (Mark 16:16). There is a difference between the people who accept Jesus Christ as their Saviour and those who voluntarily reject Him. Those who accept Him will be with Him through eternity. Those who reject Him will be lost. Whether one is cursed (damned) or blessed (saved) their state will be for eternity.

(Luke 19:22; Acts 2:23; Ephesians 6:16; II Thessalonians 2:8; Matthew 10:41; 13:43; 21:41; 25:26, 37, 46; Mark 2:17; Revelation 22:11).

The World To Come

"I looked and I saw a new heaven and a new earth" Revelation 21:1). The World to come will be new.

The shout of the archangel shall be heard and the dead in Christ shall rise. They shall not go before those who are alive, they shall be changed within the twinkling of an eye.

They shall meet Jesus Christ in the air (I Thessalonians 4:16). This will be the end of time as we know it. Sacred text (Scripture) isn't clear where this gathering place is. It will be some place in the air. The sinners will be bound to hell for a brief period. The season of Tribulation will begin and will last seven years. Then Jesus Christ and the holy people will come and reign on earth one thousand years. This will be known as the Day of the Lord. After this, they will go to the New Heaven to be with God for eternity.

(II Corinthians 12:1-4; Revelation 4:5; 21:2; Ephesians 1:20; Hebrews 8:1; 9:24; 11:10-16; 12:22, 23; 13:14).

The Resurrection

Jesus became the model for our resurrection by ascending out of the grave on Easter morning. He emerged three days after His death. His body was spiritual until the point when He rose to His Father, at that point He transformed from a spiritual body to a fleshly body, to show men the advantages and importance of this experience to the congregation.

John 20:19: peruses, "Then the same day at evening, being the first day of the week, when the doors were shut where the disciples were assembled for fear of the Jews, came Jesus and stood in the midst, and saith unto them, Peace be unto you."

This shows Jesus had a spiritual body; after His resurrection he could move toward becoming flesh when He required a body. Luke 24:39: "Behold my hands and my feet, that it is I myself; handle me, and see; for a spirit hath not flesh and bones, as ye see me have." He is now flesh and can be handled. In this resurrection He demonstrated what we will be like on the day when all will rise together to meet Jesus Christ in the air. We will have spiritual bodies. He needed to demonstrate, prove that He was Jesus the Christ. He needed to complete His earthly ministry, so He could become flesh when it was necessary.

The Resurrection is said in the Old Testament, Job 19:26: "However after my skin worms may demolish my body, yet in my substance will I see God." Psalm 49:15: "God will redeem my soul from the power of the grave; for he shall receive me." Daniel 12:2: "And many of them that rest in the dust of the earth shall awake, some to everlasting life, and some to disgrace, shame and everlasting contempt.

There was a informal resurrection on Easter and the graves opened and we have no record that they came back to the graves. Matthew 27:52: "And the graves were opened and the many bodies of the saints which slept arose."

Believe In The Resurrection

When Jesus rose from the dead, the souls of the dead waited in Hades for the resurrection.

Since Jesus passed on (died), all Christians go to Heaven. Keep in mind the criminal on the cross, to whom Jesus stated, "This day will thy leaving soul be with me in heaven" (paradise). These dead individuals who ascended with Jesus Christ had flesh bodies. They will be resurrected again on resurrection day with spiritual bodies like all other people.

There will be general resurrection day when the dead bodies and spirits will get together. John 5:28: "Marvel not at this; for the hour is coming, in which all that are in the graves shall hear his voice." Verse 29, "And shall come forth; they that have done good, unto the resurrection of life; and they that have done evil, unto the resurrection of damnation." The time isn't given. Read I Thessalonians 4:13-17" "But I would not have you to be ignorant, brethren, concerning them which are asleep, that ye sorrow not, even as others which have no hope.

For in the event that we trust that Jesus Christ died and rose once more, even so them which rest in Jesus will God carry with him. For this we say unto you by the Word of the Lord, that we which are alive and remain unto the happening to the Lord, shall not prevent them which are asleep.

For the Lord himself will descend from paradise with a shout, with the voice of the archangel and with the trump of God; and the dead in Christ will rise first. Then we which are alive and remain will be caught up together with them in the clouds, to meet the Lord in the air; and so shall we ever be with the Lord."

The great day of Resurrection will come toward the beginning of the Rapture.

(Job 19:25-27; Isaiah 26:19; Matthew 5:29; 10:28; John 5:28, 29; Romans 8:11, 22, 23).

The Tribulation

The day the Christians encounter the resurrection and go to paradise, the Holy Spirit will leave the earth. The clergymen and church will be gone so there will be no compelling reason to keep the congregation entryways open. Satan's power will wind up boundless and damnation will demonstrate its fierceness. There will howl and lashing out. The Antichrist will hold benefits similarly as he did before the Rapture.

The period before the Rapture will be difficult to continue in light of the fact that numerous weird religions will thrive and occults will draw church goers (not Christians). The Church will be so near the world that it will be difficult to tell the holy people from the sinner.

The Church will move in the direction of the divine power of desire and joy. It will work more for profit than for Salvation. The clergyman (as the shepherd) will skin the sheep rather than shear them. The Rapture will save the holy people (Christians) from this issue. This false Church will look so great it would betray those chosen by Christ, on the off chance that it were conceivable.

On the day the Tribulation begins, the seals will be opened and all that is depicted will start to happen. The lesson on the seals might be found in Revelation 6:1-17. The serious part will last just three and a half years since God will intercede on the grounds that the people who oppose the Antichrist and the beast can't endure through any more.

The test for the redeemed of this period will be numerous scars on the body. The people who can't take it can submit themselves to the

Antichrist and have the sign of the beast put on their foreheads. The individuals who joined the brute will be thrown into damnation. This hellfire won't be the perpetual place. After the Millennium, there will be incredible day of atonement. The Saints will go to the new Heaven and the sinners will go to damnation (hell); this will resemble a lake that consumes with flame and brimstone. The Jews who rejected Jesus Christ are as yet alive at the Rapture will have an opportunity to acknowledge and accept Him. The Bible reveals to us that some will be saved amid this period.

Try not to wait! Acknowledge and accept the Savior today by giving your life to Jesus Christ. (Isaiah 2:5-22; 16:1-5; 24:1-25; Jeremiah 303-11; Zechariah 12:10-13; Revelation 6:1-19; Romans 11:26-29; Matthew 23:39; 24:15-31; Luke 17:22-27; II Timothy 3:1-12).

The Second Coming Of Jesus Christ

"For the Son of man will come in the glory of his Father with his holy angels; and then he shall reward each man as per his works!" (Matthew 16:27)

The Bible is positive in expressing that Jesus is coming back once more. The day and hour are obscure. He will come as a thief or looter.

Researchers concur that the Resurrection and the Rapture will come together. The resurrected bodies will meet Jesus Christ in the air.

Numerous Bible instructors concur that the Tribulation will take after the Rapture and end with the Second Coming of Jesus Christ. Others say the Rapture and the Resurrection have traveled every which way, and we are living in the Tribulation now. They say the Church never again has capacity to change society, it has turned into another foundation in the public eye attempting to remain in business; just the business isn't unmistakably characterized. The Holy Ghost (or Holy Spirit) is never again doing His work of keeping persons holy. The new birth isn't evolving anyone. The transgressions of men are defiling the Church. The music is never again sacrosanct (holy, godly); the rock and move beat has been received. The objective of music in the Church is for amusement and passionate inebriation.

We trust that there are individuals who have been born again in each congregation. There are some genuine Christians who are worried about the Salvation of others. The Holy Spirit is doing His work through the persons who have submitted themselves to Jesus Christ. The music in a few holy places is holy and intended to help spread the Gospel and motivate Christians to a higher feeling of obligation.

The Second Coming of Jesus Christ is in the future. Jesus will come after the Tribulation and set the earth in order. He will destroy the Antichrist, put Satan under subjection and destroy death. He will call from the grave the people who progressed toward becoming Christians amid the Tribulation that got killed and change the bodies of those who moved toward becoming Christians and are alive at the Second Coming.

Jesus Christ made His Second Coming sound so pressing to His disciples that they sold out all that they had and went out to save the world. They didn't trust that they would confront passing on, however would go from this life to glory. We know they died doing their work for the Master.

When He comes He will judge everybody that lived and the redeemed will rule with Him as He leads from David's position of authority. This implies He will be in Jerusalem. Read Matthew 24:29; Revelation 19:11-21; and Revelation 20:1-10.

He will begin the Millennium and the holy people who were slaughtered for the Church will reign with Him. The devil and those who rejected Him will be headed in hellfire for one thousand years. Toward the millennium's end, the earth and the heaven will pass away and another heaven and earth will have their place.

Jesus Christ will leave the earth with every one of the Saints (Christians) and go to paradise (heaven) to rule until the end of time. You should be prepared to rule with Him. He that believeth and is purified through water, will be saved, and the Christians will be with God until the end of time. (Matthew 24:36; Mark 13:32; Luke 12:40; `17:26-30; 24:21; Revelation 1:6-15; I Corinthians 4:5; 11:26; 15:23; Romans 11:15-32; 22:2-9; Daniel 2:35, 44; I Thessalonians 2:19; 3:13; 4:15; II Peter 3:3, 4).

Bibliography

Agnew, M.S. (1980) The Holy Spirit: Friend And Counselor. Kansas City, MO.: **Beacon Hill Press**

Grimmett, J. F. (1980) The Presupposition Of Revelation. Nashville, TN.: **Publisher Unkown.**

Hyatt, J. H. (1964) The Heritage Of Biblical Faith. Saint Louis, MI.: The Bethany **Press**

Ryrie, C C. (1965) The Holy Spirit. Chicago, Ill.: The Moody Press

Stewart, J. S. (1959) The Life And Teachings Of Jesus Christ. New York, NY.: **Abingdon Press**

Wiley, H. O. (1952) Christian Theology, Vol. III. Kansas City, MO.: Beacon Hill **Press**

Funk & Wagnalls Standard Dictionary (Comprehensive) International Edition, **Vol. I. Chicago, Ill.: J. G. Ferguson**

The New Combined Bible Dictionary And Concordance (1984). Dallas, TX.: **American Evangelistic Association**

The New Testament In Modern English (1958) New York, NY.: London, UK.: **J. B. Phillips, Simon & Schuster (Used By Permission)**

The New Testament In The Language Of The People (1937, 1949) Chicago, Ill.: **Charles B. Williams, Bruce Humphries Inc., Moody Bible Institute (Used By Permission)**

The Holy Bible (1964) Authorized King James Version. Chicago, Ill.: J. G. **Ferguson**

The Holy Bible (1953) The Revised Standard Version. Nashville, TN.: Nelson & **Sons (Used BY Permission)**

The Holy Bible (1901) The American Standard
Version. Nashville, TN.: Thomas
Nelson (Used By Permission)

The Holy Bible (1959) The Berkeley Version.
Grand Rapids, MI.: Zondervan (Used
By Permission)

The Wycliff Bible Commentary (1962)
Nashville, TN.: The Southwestern Company,
The Moody Bible Institute Of Chicago

ABOUT THE AUTHOR

The Reverend Dr. John Thomas Wylie is one who has dedicated his life to the work of God's Service, the service of others; and being a powerful witness for the Gospel of Our Lord and Savior Jesus Christ. Dr. Wylie was called into the Gospel Ministry June 1979, whereby in that same year he entered The American Baptist College of the American Baptist Theological Seminary, Nashville, Tennessee.

As a young Seminarian, he read every book available to him that would help him better his understanding of God as well as God's plan of Salvation and the Christian Faith. He made a commitment as a promising student that he would inspire others as God inspires him. He understood early in his ministry that we live in times where people question not only who God is; but whether miracles are real, whether or not man can make a change, and who the enemy is or if the enemy truly exists.

Dr. Wylie carried out his commitment to God, which has been one of excellence which led to his earning his Bachelors of Arts in Bible/ Theology/Pastoral Studies. Faithful and obedient to the call of God, he continued to matriculate in his studies earning his Masters of Ministry from Emmanuel Bible College, Nashville, Tennessee & Emmanuel Bible College, Rossville, Georgia. Still, inspired to please the Lord and do that which is well – pleasing in the Lord's sight, Dr. Wylie recently on March 2006, completed his Masters of Education degree with a concentration in Instructional Technology earned at The American Intercontinental University, Holloman Estates, Illinois. Dr. Wylie also previous to this, earned his Education Specialist Degree from Jones International University, Centennial, Colorado and his Doctorate of Theology from The Holy Trinity College and Seminary, St. Petersburg, Florida.

Dr. Wylie has served in the capacity of pastor at two congregations in Middle Tennessee and Southern Tennessee, as well as served as an

Evangelistic Preacher, Teacher, Chaplain, Christian Educator, and finally a published author, writer of many great inspirational Christian Publications such as his first publication: *"Only One God: Who Is*

He?" – published August 2002 via formally 1st books library (which is now AuthorHouse Book Publishers located in Bloomington, Indiana & Milton Keynes, United Kingdom) which caught the attention of **The Atlanta Journal Constitution Newspaper.**

Dr. Wylie is happily married to Angel G. Wylie, a retired Dekalb Elementary School teacher who loves to work with the very young children and who always encourages her husband to move forward in the Name of Jesus Christ. They have Four children, 11 grand-children and one great-grandson of whom they are very proud. Both Dr. Wylie and Angela Wylie serve as members of the Salem Baptist Church, located in Lilburn, Georgia, where the Reverend Dr. Richard B. Haynes is Senior pastor.

Dr. Wylie has stated of his wife: "she knows the charm and beauty of sincerity, goodness, and purity through Jesus Christ. Yes, she is a Christian and realizes the true meaning of loveliness as the reflection as her life of holy living gives new meaning, hope, and purpose to that of her husband, her children, others may say of her, "Behold the handmaiden of the Lord." A Servant of Jesus Christ!